MOTHER COURAGE AND HER CHILDREN

Bertolt Brecht

AUTHORED by Robert William
UPDATED AND REVISED by Adam Kissel

COVER DESIGN by Table XI Partners LLC
COVER PHOTO by Olivia Verma and © 2005 GradeSaver, LLC

BOOK DESIGN by Table XI Partners LLC

Published by GradeSaver LLC, www.gradesaver.com

First published in the United States of America by GradeSaver LLC. 2007

ISBN 978-1-60259-101-1

Printed in the United States of America

For other products and additional information please visit http://www.gradesaver.com

Table of Contents

Table of Contents

Biography of Bertolt Brecht (1898-1956)

Bertolt Brecht was born on February 10, 1898, in the medieval city of Augsburg, part of the Bavarian section of the German Empire. Married in 1897, his father was a Catholic and his mother a Protestant. Brecht was their first child, baptized as Eugen Bertolt Friedrich Brecht. His father, Bertolt Friedrich Brecht, worked in a paper factory. His mother, Wilhelmine Friederike Sophie Brezing, was ill with breast cancer most of his young life. He had one brother, Walter, who was born in 1900.

Brecht was a sickly child, having a congenital heart condition and a facial tic. As a result he was sent to a sanitarium to relax. At age six he attended a Protestant elementary school (Volksschule) and at age ten a private school, The Royal Bavarian Realgymnasium (Koeniglich-Bayerisches Realgymnasium). Like most students, he was educated in Latin and the humanities, later being exposed to Nietzsche and other thinkers. He suffered a heart attack at the age of twelve but soon recovered and continued his education.

Significantly, Brecht was exposed at a young age to Luther's German translation of the Bible, a text considered instrumental in the development of the modern German language. Quotes from and references to the Bible abound throughout Brecht's work and can be found most particularly in **Mother Courage and Her Children** in the mouth of the chaplain.

While in school he began writing, and he ended up co-founding and co-editing a school magazine called *The Harvest*. By age sixteen he was writing for a local newspaper and had written his first play, The Bible, about a girl who must choose between living and dying but saving many others. He was later almost expelled at age eighteen for dissenting about it being necessary to defend his country in time of war. By nineteen he had left school and started doing clerical work for the war, prevented from more active duty due to health problems.

In 1917 he resumed his education, this time attending Ludwig Maximilian Universitaet in Munich, where he matriculated as a medical student. By this time his mother was heavily drugged with morphine as a result of her progressing cancer. He started to write *Baal* at this time, a play concerned with suffering caused by excessive sexual pleasures. It sensationally depicted what were considered immoral attitudes at the time.

Brecht's own sex life is fascinating in many ways. He is thought to have had no fewer than three mistresses at any time throughout his adult life. When he was a child, the family's second servant, Marie Miller, would hide objects in her undergarments for Brecht and his brother to search for. Through Brecht's poetry we understand that his mother used to smell his clothes to determine the extent of his sexual activities. By the age of sixteen he began to frequent a brothel as part of a conscientious effort to broaden his experiences. Between sixteen and twenty he apparently pursued eight girls simultaneously, including Paula Banholzer, the woman who gave birth to his illegitimate child in 1919. He is known to have experimented with homosexuality, often inviting literary and musically inclined male friends to his room on weekends in order for them to read erotic compositions. His diaries, although vague, mention his need for both males and females to fulfill his sexual desires. Brecht's desire for experience was, throughout his life, all-consuming.

In 1921 he took his second trip to Berlin and attended the rehearsals of Max Reinhardt and other major directors. In 1922 his play *Drums in the Night* opened in Munich at the Kammerspiele and later at the Deutsches Theater in Berlin. He received the prestigious Kleist prize for young dramatists as a result. Brecht also entered into his first committed relationship, his marriage with the opera singer Marianne Zoff, at the age of twenty-four. Their daughter Hanne was born the following year. Despite being married, Brecht had extramarital affairs and spent very little time with his wife or daughter. In 1923 his two plays Jungle of Cities and *Baal* were performed.

After moving to Berlin in 1924, he met a communist Viennese actress, Helene Weigel. His wife Marianne moved in with her parents after the birth of Hanne, and soon she stopped responding to Brecht's letters. At age twenty-six Brecht fathered his second illegitimate child, with Weigel. Their son was named Stefan. Brecht divorced Marianne Zoff and in 1929 married Helene Weigel. At this point he was just thirty-one.

Helene Weigel gave birth to their second child, Barbara, in 1930. During this time Brecht was by no means monogamous. He was obsessed with the idea of abandonment, and as a result he abhorred ending relationships. The women in his life were important for his writing career, and modern feminist detractors often try to claim that his mistresses in fact wrote much of what he takes credit for. The allegation is largely untrue. But women such as Elisabeth Hauptmann did write significant parts of The Threepenny Opera, and other mistresses included Margarete Steffin, who helped him write *The Good Woman of Sezuan* and Mother Courage and Her Children; Hella Wuolijoki, who allowed him to transform her comedy *The Sawdust Princess* into *Herr Puntila and His Man Matti*; and Ruth Berlau, who at least bore him a short-lived, third illegitimate child in 1944. Weigel was tolerant of his affairs, and she even warned other men to stay away from his mistresses on account of it upsetting him when they made their moves.

Brecht's writings show the profound influence of many varied sources during this time and the remaining years of his life. He studied Chinese, Japanese, and Indian theatre, focused heavily on Shakespeare (adapting, among other plays, Shakespeare's *Coriolanus*) and other Elizabethans, and was fascinated by Greek tragedy. He found inspiration in other German playwrights, notably Buchner and Wedekind, and he enjoyed the Bavarian folk play. Mother Courage and Her Children arguably owes much to Schiller's *Wallenstein* trilogy. Brecht had a phenomenal ability to take elements from these seemingly incompatible sources, combine them, and convert them into his own works.

In 1933 Brecht took his family and fled to Zurich after the burning of the Reichstag, later moving around the world to escape Nazi rule. In October 1947, during the McCarthy years, Brecht was called to appear before the House Committee on Un-American Activities. Although not an official member of America's communist party, Brecht left the United States for Switzerland the next day. He soon reunited with Helene Weigel, and they traveled to East Berlin in 1948 and set up the Berliner Ensemble with full support from the communist regime. Mother Courage and Her Children was the Berliner Ensemble's inaugural production. In 1950, Brecht and Weigel were granted Austrian citizenship.

Brecht's four great plays were written between 1938 and 1945. These included, for one, *The Life of Galileo*, which followed history all too slavishly. It dealt with the protagonist's self-hatred for giving up his convictions in the face of the Inquisition. The others were Mother Courage and Her Children; *The Good Person of Sezuan*, which in some ways follows from Mother Courage in examining the compatibility of virtue and a capitalist world; and The Caucasian Chalk Circle, which introduces questions about power and who is entitled to own things. After this period, Brecht worked on his famous adaptation of *Antigone* and spent much of his energy recording his theoretical ideas.

Brecht experimented with dada and expressionism in his early plays, but he soon developed a unique style which suited his own vision. He detested "Aristotelian" drama and the manner in which it (at least from his point of view) made the audience identify with the hero without enough analysis of the hero's flaws. To him, when such drama produced feelings of terror and pity and led to an emotional catharsis, the process prevented audience members from thinking. (It is the ancient quarrel between philosophers and poets once again, with another thinker trying to reform poetry.) Determined to destroy what he took to be theatrical illusions, Brecht made his dreams into realities when he took over the Berliner Ensemble. In one of his early productions, he famously put up signs which said, "Glotzt nicht so romantisch!" (Don't stare so romantically!). For further information, see *About Epic Theatre* in the ClassicNote on Mother Courage and Her Children.

Brecht received the National Prize, first class, in 1951. In 1954 he won the international Lenin Peace Prize. Brecht died of a heart attack on August 14, 1956, while working on a response to Samuel Beckett's absurdist play Waiting for Godot, written the year before. Even at the end, Brecht was very much interested in the modern drama of the day. He provided instructions that a stiletto be placed in his heart and that he be buried in a steel coffin so that his corpse would not be riddled with worms. He also left a will giving the proceeds of his various works to particular mistresses, including Elisabeth Hauptmann and Ruth Berlau. Unfortunately for them, the will lacked the necessary witness signatures and was therefore considered void. His widow, Helene Weigel, generously gave small amounts of money to the specified women. Brecht is buried in the Dorotheenfriedhof in Berlin.

About Mother Courage and Her Children

Mother Courage and Her Children is set during the Thirty Years' War, but it was written either shortly before or during the early years of the Second World War. Hitler's warmongering intentions had become clear to many Germans by the mid-1930s, and Brecht himself, already opposed to the man he called "the great bandit," had repeatedly emigrated so as to escape the rise of fascism. "The dark times" was how Brecht referred to this era in his writing, and it is against the backdrop of the rise of Hitler that the play was written.

Brecht lived until April 1939 in Denmark, where in 1938 he had written *Fear and Misery in the Third Reich*, a series of short scenes which demonstrated without restraint the degree of horror that would ensue, so he prophesied, should the Nazis come to power. Today, they serve as a blistering warning which all too obviously fell on deaf ears. After Denmark, Brecht moved to Sweden. This is where Mother Courage and Her Children was first drafted. The decision to write the play was taken after Hitler and Stalin had signed their rather improbable pact. Brecht wrote that

> this pact makes the air clearer. what we have is a war between imperialist states. we have germany as the aggressor and warmonger. we have aggressive capitalism against defensive capitalism.

We can see clearly from these lines the impetus for the play's war of religion that actually has nothing to do with religion.

The play was written with the intention that Naima Wifstrand, a Swedish actress, would play Mother Courage, and his wife Helene Weigel would be Kattrin (since she spoke no Swedish). Although it was written in Sweden, the play is set in the Germany of the past, and it is concerned with the Germany of Brecht's present. Brecht's decision to set his play in the Germany of the past, the Thirty Years' War, underlines several of the impulses behind his writing the play itself. The Thirty Years' War remains one of the most significant conflicts in German history. C. V. Wedgewood's account of it, much read by students of history when it was published in 1938, was re-published after the Second World War with a foreword which recognized that

> the dismal course of this war still seems to me to be an object lesson on the dangers ... which can arise when men of ... little minds are in high places.

The same lesson could be inferred from Brecht's play. Brecht was not interested in history per se but in the fact that history seemed to be repeating itself: the play itself is a warning against the capitalism which, Brecht believed, drove both the war of the play and the war he was living through. The war, Brecht believed, "teaches mankind about itself, as it were, it reads a lesson, a text to which the thunder of gunfire and the exploding bombs merely provide the accompaniment." Observing from his own international distance, Brecht's home country seemed to be catastrophically failing to learn the lesson its past was reading to it.

Brecht had to move to America to escape Hitler, and--though he escaped successfully--this move hugely delayed the possibility of the production of the play. The critical audience that Brecht so desired simply did not yet exist. An examination of the play's stage history shows how, across the globe, Mother Courage and Her Children took some years to find its foothold in the popular theater. This, perhaps more than anything else, was because of the way it so absolutely broke with contemporary theatrical tradition, both in its brutal presentation of war and in its inauguration of "Epic Theatre," the first step toward a new kind of international theater. After several failed attempts to get it performed, it was not until Brecht's return to Germany that the first production, by invitation of Wolfgang Langhoff, Intendant of the Deutsches Theater, was planned for 1949. It had made little impact so far, but the 1949 production not only would severely rock the boat of European theater, but it also would introduce the world to the ideas and theories of Bertolt Brecht.

Character List

Mother Courage

The title character, her real name is Anna Fierling. She earned her name Mother Courage in Riga when she ran through a bombardment in order to sell her loaves of bread. She has three children, Eilif, Swiss Cheese, and Kattrin, whom she tries to take care of and protect throughout the play. She loses all three children while following the war around Europe and ends the play alone with her wagon.

Mother Courage is a deeply contradictory character: courageous, forthright, and intelligent, yet fatally unable to forgo her trade in order to protect her children. Brecht attempts, by the end of the play, to make her seem deeply unsympathetic. At the close of the play, when she insists she must "get back into business," we realise that she has learned nothing. The war has ruined her, but it has failed to teach her, and Brecht's play desperately attempts to teach the audience by showing what Mother Courage never learns.

Mother Courage was originally played by Helene Weigel in Brecht's original production, and her achievement remains a major challenge to today's actresses. The character is one of very few unsympathetic major female parts in modern drama.

Kattrin

Mother Courage's daughter. Kattrin is a teenage girl, and the play details her awakening (and repressed) sexual desires. Initially she is promised that she can have a husband in peacetime, though she is disfigured by an assault in Scene 6. She thus is obsessed with babies and small children.

Kattrin is a mute, but ironically she is one of the play's most emotionally eloquent characters. In the play's penultimate scene, she is killed as she attempts to warn a town about an imminent siege. She bears out one of Brecht's favorite sayings: "silence sometimes makes the most noise."

Eilif

Mother Courage's eldest and favorite son, he is something of a thug, though she thinks him "dashing" and "brave." He is recruited by the Recruiting Officer in the first scene, and he seems after that to really enjoy the war. Much praised by the General in Scene 2 for slaughtering peasants and stealing their livestock, Eilif is executed for committing the same deed in Scene 6 in peacetime. Mother Courage never knows of his death.

Swiss Cheese

Mother Courage's younger son. Swiss Cheese is, according to his mother, too honest. He is painted by Brecht to be rather stupid. He takes a job as paymaster of the Second Finnish Regiment and attempts to hide its cashbox so that he can return it to his general after the Catholics have gained power. He is caught with it and shortly executed.

Cook

The cook for the Swedish General. He first appears when Mother Courage haggles with him over the price of a capon, and he becomes her sexual partner later in the play. He is "Peter the Puff," the man whom Yvette Pottier fell in love with, thereby causing her to follow the army as a prostitute for five years.

His name, rather aptly chosen, is "Lamb," which bears out his treatment in Scene 2--and his eventual going AWOL. When the food runs out, a cook is only a sacrificial lamb.

He is deeply cynical. He is perhaps best summed up by his line "what is, is" (*was ist, ist*). He is out for what he can get from the war, and at the end of the play he parts company with Mother Courage when she declines his offer of co-running his newly acquired inn in Utrecht.

Chaplain

An army chaplain and a personification of Brecht's view that religion is of no use when it comes to war. He is a total coward and a hypocrite, switching religious allegiance with the twirl of a clerical robe, and throughout the play he seems bitter if not also rather smarmy. He complains throughout the play that his clerical talents are going to waste, yet the virtues that we might expect from a religious man seem permanently absent in him.

Yvette Pottier

A prostitute in the army, she follows the army after falling in love with the Cook. After the Catholics arrest Swiss Cheese, she picks up a colonel and convinces him to give her money with which to buy Mother Courage's wagon. In the end, Swiss Cheese's death means that the deal does not go forward.

She reappears later in the play, having married the same colonel's brother, now much older and fatter, but rich. She has sold herself completely to the war, but for a good price. She is the only person who gains from the war--at only the price of her beauty.

Recruiting Officer

The man who recruits Eilif in Scene 1. He has the sergeant distract Mother Courage with the promise of a sale and takes Eilif away with him, promising him beer, new clothes, and the glamor of danger.

Sergeant

The man who distracts Mother Courage so that her son Eilif can be recruited into the army.

Swedish General

The leader of the Swedish Regiment, he is introduced in Scene Two. Mother Courage overhears him congratulating Eilif for Eilif's bravery. She claims that he must be a bad commander after hearing him tell Eilif that he needs more "brave" men, since if he had good battle plans, there would be no need for bravery.

Munitions Officer

Introduced in Scene 3, he sells Mother Courage a bag of bullets.

Man with the Eyepatch

An informer for the Catholic Army, he attempts to investigate Swiss Cheese's possession of the 2nd Finnish Regiment's cashbox. He spots Swiss Cheese hiding the cash box and arrests him. Puppeteered by Mother Courage, Yvette tries to bribe him to release Swiss Cheese, but the haggling takes too long, and Swiss Cheese is killed. (See Scene 3.)

Another Sergeant

An officer in the Catholic Army, he helps arrest Swiss Cheese after Swiss Cheese tries to hide the regimental cash box.

Old Colonel

A regimental leader, he is very old. Yvette "picks" him up and convinces him to give her the money to buy Mother Courage's wagon. He pretends to be her "financial advisor" and talks to her as one might talk to a small child. He is one of the many high-powered grotesques of the play.

Clerk

The clerk is in charge of the complaint station, where Mother Courage goes to complain about the way the soldiers messed up her wagon.

Young Soldier

A young man who is furious that his sergeant stole some reward money that he should have gotten for rescuing the colonel's horse from the river. He waits with Mother Courage outside the tent. Mother Courage sings to him "The Song of the Great Capitulation," which leads to him storming out. (See Scene 5.)

Older Soldier

An older man who accompanies the Young Soldier to the complaint tent in Scene 5, attempting to restrain him.

Peasant

A man wounded in Scene 5 during the battle, he has lost his arm and needs bandages. He tells the chaplain that his child is still in the house, causing Kattrin to rush in and save the baby. Mother Courage refuses to provide bandages until the chaplain forcefully removes her from the wagon and takes some of her shirts.

Peasant Woman

A woman wounded in Scene 5. She is concerned about her farm and the fact that her family has lost everything.

Young Man

A young man who tries to sell bedding feathers to Mother Courage in Scene 8. He takes his mother home after peace is declared.

Old Woman

An old woman who tries to sell bedding to Mother Courage in Scene 8; she faints when peace is declared and then leaves with her son to return home.

Voice

A voice that invites the Cook and Mother Courage to come inside the parsonage for some soup. There is also a voice that sings the "Song of Plenty" in Scene 10.

Peasants

At the farmhouse in Scene 11, the peasants agree to work with the Catholic soldiers in besieging the town of Halle. They are mortified when Kattrin takes a drum and beats it on the roof of their farmhouse. They eventually are paid by Mother Courage to bury her body in Scene 12.

Lieutenant

The man in charge of infiltrating Halle and killing off the residents. He orders the soldiers to shoot with a harquebus and kill Kattrin while she is on the roof.

Major Themes

Lower Classes During Wartime

From the first image--a nameless "Sergeant" and "Recruiting Officer" freezing in a field--Brecht's play sets its focus firmly on the lower classes affected by wars. No historically significant figures (General Tilly or the Kaiser, for example) make appearances in the play, being mentioned only in passing. Mother Courage, her family, and her companions are all the "little people," and it is their story which Brecht finds interesting. They usually are unable to extract any benefit from the war. Notice, too, how often minor characters in the play are given only a profession or a description rather than a proper name: we have peasants, numerous soldiers, generals, clerks, captains, officers, and even chaplains. This is not just because they are stock characters.

Key scenes to analyze in writing about this theme: Scenes 1, 5, 11, and 12.

Courage

"Parachutists are dropped like bombs," Brecht once wrote, "and bombs do not need courage. Real courage would be refusing to get into the plane in the first place." This idea points toward the remarkable irony with which Mother Courage's nickname is imbued. That is, the play suggests that her courage is as questionable as her motherhood. She gets her nickname from driving loaves through the bombardment of Riga before they become too moldy (see Scene 1), but this might be rashness rather than true courage. Moreover, in light of Brecht's lines above, real courageousness seems to involve opting out of the war and its capitalism altogether, something Mother Courage never does, although it is hard to see her alternatives as one of the "little people."

Mother Courage herself seems to see this idea: real courage requires persistence enough to make a significant, life-threatening change, as Kattrin does at the end of Scene 11. Consider when Mother Courage advises the young soldier about the Great Capitulation in Scene 4--but this insight does not survive with her to the end of the play.

Key scenes to analyze in writing about this theme: Scenes 1, 2, 4, and 11.

Families and Parenthood

The play examines war not just as a capitalistic system but also on a domestic level. It is central to the emotional impact of the play that it is about a mother and her children. Mother Courage's treatment of (particularly) Kattrin and Swiss Cheese emphasizes the difficulty of combining her role of "mother" with her professional role of "canteen woman." One of the play's key questions is whether her trading helps or hinders her family--it is the only way for them to survive, but it results in the deaths of all of her children. Significantly, whenever one of the children die, Brecht ensures that Mother Courage is distracted by business affairs.

It also is interesting to examine Kattrin's journey (as by far the most important of the children) through the play in light of how far her development, desires, and growing sexuality are repressed and damaged by the fact that her mother is a wartime canteen woman.

Key scenes to analyze in writing about this theme: Scenes 1, 3, 9, 11, and 12.

War as Capitalism

Brecht was a lifelong socialist. After the First World War, the idea began to become more popular that war was often associated with financial gain. From this point of view, Brecht's purpose in writing the play was to show that in wartime "you need a big pair of scissors in order to get your cut." War, as the play portrays it, is itself a capitalist system designed to make profit for just a few players, and it is perpetuated for that purpose.

Therefore, despite the fact that she is constantly trying to make profit from it, Mother Courage is destined to lose by trading during the war; only the fat cats at the top of the system have a real chance of profiting from it. People in this play are always looking to get their cut, large or small, and it is no accident that the original text repeats the verb *kriegen*, to "wage"--that is, to wage war (*Krieg*), but also meaning to "get" or "acquire."

Key scenes to analyze in writing about this theme: Scenes 1, 3, and 7.

Silence and Dumbness

Kattrin's dumbness is deeply symbolic. That is, real virtue and goodness are silenced in the time of war. Brecht even makes clear that Kattrin's dumbness is due directly to the war: "a soldier stuck something in her mouth when she was small." The play itself deals similarly with several significant silences: Mother Courage's refusal to complain after the Song of the Great Capitulation, the chaplain's denial of his own faith when the Catholics arrive in Scene 3 ("All good Catholics here!"), and the way Mother Courage denies her own son at the end of the scene, first in life and then in death. Weigel's silent scream at the end of this scene is itself an emblem of how war neuters human response.

An antithesis to dumbness is eloquence, and Kattrin's death (itself conducted through loud noises, and answered by the noises from the town after she has died) is perhaps the single most eloquent act in the play.

Key scenes to analyze in writing about this theme: Scenes 3, 6, and 11.

Tragedy

A common critical discussion about the play is whether or not it is a tragedy. Brecht perhaps did not write it as one, titling his play "A Chronicle of the Thirty Years' War" and aiming to make connections to contemporary issues. But some critics have argued that, in line with Brecht's guidance about Mother Courage's failure to learn, the play is perhaps Mother Courage's tragedy. After all, her children die and she never profits appreciably from the war.

Such a discussion depends much on how "tragedy" is defined. For instance, it is worth noting that, in addition to Mother Courage's failure to learn, Brecht assigns each of her children a "tragic flaw" which is repeated throughout the play: Eilif is "dashing," Swiss Cheese is "honest," and Kattrin "suffers from pity."

To research this theme more, after reading a theoretical work on tragedy (such as Aristotle's *Poetics*), one could ask the following questions: is Mother Courage herself responsible for the events of the play? That is, would events go differently if only Mother Courage were different? Does the play arouse a *catharsis* as the curtain comes down? Is the play merely sad or a true tragedy?

Key scenes to analyze in writing about this theme: Scenes 1, 4, 6, and 12.

Religion

Brecht's view of religion in this play is blatantly clear: it is of little help, and is often a hindrance, during wartime. Religion is portrayed through the sniveling, hypocritical figure of the Chaplain, and it has little positive role to play. The Chaplain changes his allegiances (for example, dusting out his clerical robes when peace is announced) at the drop of a hat (see Scene 6 for the point at which his character becomes clearest). At the very end, the prayers of the peasants are juxtaposed with Kattrin climbing the rooftop, suggesting ineffective inaction among the religious versus effective action by Kattrin.

The text, like all of Brecht's work, is steeped in a complex knowledge of the Old Testament, but the play itself makes little concession to religion as a positive influence on society.

Key scenes to analyze in writing about this theme: Scenes 2, 3, 6, and 8.

War as Order

In the first scene, there is a grotesque description of how the citizens of the world rely on war to hold civilization together. An audience member might be forgiven for dismissing it as an opening joke. Yet, the idea of war as order, "peace as war undeclared," as the Chaplain has it--recurs throughout, and the Chaplain believably expresses very similar sentiments at various points in the play.

Mother Courage herself is an emblem of the way the play's society seems to depend upon the perpetuity of war and, for the brief time while peace is declared, peace is often described as a disaster rather than the end of a devastating war. Is war actually the axis on which the society of the play turns? Is the nature of man antagonistic rather than cooperative?

Key scenes to analyze in writing about this theme: Scenes 1, 5, 6, 7, and 8.

Feeding the War

Scene 2, outside and inside the General's kitchen, introduces the Cook and the idea of "feeding the war." The Cook's name is "Lamb," and though he becomes a sacrificial lamb later in the play when the food runs out, the idea of being a lamb also suggests a way that his role reflects the mission of the whole army. The play opens with a conversation between a sergeant and a recruiting officer about how difficult it is to find enough soldiers to fill the quota--the war's appetite is greater than the available resources can satisfy. The Cook and the whole army feed society's appetite for war.

Throughout the play, nevertheless, starvation recurs. The lack of men in Scene 1 becomes the more literal lack of good meat in Scene 2. The lack of such food, by the bleak ending of the play, has become manifest across the whole country. In Scene 9, trade has had to stop because food is no longer growing.

Key scenes to analyze in writing about this theme: Scenes 1, 2, 8, and 9.

Glossary of Terms

Alienation

Epic Theatre insisted that its spectators were to engage critically with the action more than engaging with it emotionally. "Alienation" was the term used for this critical "detachment." The point was not merely to be alienated from one's emotions. In German, *Verfremdung* ("alienation") means "to make strange," and from this root one can see how making events seem strange or "alien" might provoke thinking, the critical detachment that Brecht so advocated.

Capitalism

An economic system whereby profit is a primary motive for trade; that is, investors employ capital (money) in order to make more money. The term is also used to refer to a political ideology that supports economic capitalism, whereby state control of industry is considered anti-individual and free exchange is promoted even at the expense of common social interests.

Capitulation

Giving in or succumbing. It often is a military term describing when soldiers surrender. Mother Courage's use of the term in Scene 4 points out how everyone in the play eventually gives in to the larger capitalist system of the war.

Capon

A male chicken whose reproductive organs were removed at an early age, in order that it could be fattened for eating.

Chaplain

A member of the clergy who does not serve an organized congregation or church, often found in universities, in hospitals, and (as here) in armies.

Christ's Passion

The theological term for the suffering of Jesus during the hours prior to and during his crucifixion.

Couragemodell (the "model")

Brecht invented a new method of direction, though it never particularly caught on. He proposed that playwrights would record all of their decisions as they prepared for the original performances of their work, from actors' intonations to the lighting and stage blocking. Thus, future directors could study this "model" production in order to understand the author's and the play's aims and intended interpretations--before forming their own versions for performance. Theatrically, Brecht's model has served to set his play in stone rather than release it as a

Platonic ideal with secular instantiations from one director to the next. Thus, from a literary point of view, it is fascinating to get a fine-grained picture of the play as Brecht intended it and had it performed.

Dramatic Theater

The opposite of what Brecht called epic theater, that is, a derogatory term used by Brecht as well as a theater tradition. Brecht thought that the "dramatic theater" had its primary goal to move or excite its audience, which to him was not a "noble" enough aim for the theater.

Epic Theater

A theater movement created by Brecht and having the primary goal of educating the audience, that is, leading them to analyze critically what they watch rather than simply being emotionally involved in it.

General Tilly (1559-1632)

A field marshal who commanded the armies of the Imperial and Holy Roman Empire during the Thirty Years' War.

Harquebus

A primitive firearm used in the 15th to 17th centuries.

Kriegen

The German verb to "wage war" (*Krieg kriegen*), with the secondary meaning to "get" or "get hold of." This is a telling double meaning for the interpretation of this play. The verb recurs throughout the play.

Looting

Stealing goods. In this play, it involves robbing from the townspeople after a town has been besieged.

Shot

Ammunition or bullets, usually (though not exclusively) for a musket.

Thirty Years' War (1618-1648)

A major European conflict, fought mostly in what is now Germany, which began as a civil war with religious roots and quickly became (as Brecht emphasizes) an international war of religion between Catholic and Protestant powers. It ended with a new world order determined by the major powers on hand in Europe at the Peace of Westphalia.

Short Summary

The play is set in Europe during the Thirty Years' War. Mother Courage, a canteen woman, pulls her cart with her three children (Eilif, Kattrin, and Swiss Cheese) in the wake of the army, trading with the soldiers and attempting to make profit from the war.

We are first introduced to a Recruiting Officer and a Sergeant, who complain about the difficulty of recruiting soldiers for the war. Mother Courage's cart is pulled on and, distracting her with the promise of a transaction, the Recruiting Officer leads Eilif off. One of her children is now gone.

Two years later, we find Mother Courage haggling with the General's Cook over a capon. On the other side of the stage, Eilif is praised by the General for heroically slaughtering some peasants and stealing their cattle. Eilif sings "The Song of the Girl and the Soldier," and his mother joins in. She then berates him for risking his life so stupidly.

Three years later, Swiss Cheese has taken a job as the regiment's paymaster. Yvette Pottier, the camp prostitute, sings "The Song of Fraternization" to warn Kattrin about the horrors of a relationship with a soldier. The Cook and the Chaplain arrive to greet Mother Courage with a message from Eilif, and there is suddenly a Catholic attack. The Chaplain discards his robes, and Swiss Cheese hides the regiment's paybox.

Later the same evening, Swiss Cheese is followed when he attempts to return the paybox to his General but is captured. Mother Courage mortgages her cart to Yvette and tries to bargain with the soldiers using the money--but she bargains for too long, and Swiss Cheese is shot. Mother Courage denies his body when it is brought to her to be identified, so it is thrown into a pit.

The next scene finds Mother Courage waiting to complain outside the Captain's tent. She sings the "Song of the Great Capitulation" to a young soldier who also has come to complain to the Captain. The song, which has the moral "everyone gives in sooner or later," leads to the soldier's storming out, and Courage herself ends up deciding that she doesn't want to complain.

On the day of the funeral of General Tilly, Mother Courage undertakes a stock check, and she talks at length with the Chaplain about whether or not the war will continue. He convinces her that it will, so she decides to invest in more stock for her cart. The Chaplain suggests that Mother Courage could marry him, but he is rejected. Kattrin appears and returns to her mother, severely disfigured, having collected some merchandise. Mother Courage thus curses the war.

In the following brief scene, Courage sings a song that praises the war as a good provider. Business is good for now.

Two peasants wake up Mother Courage, trying to sell her some bedding, shortly before the news breaks that peace has broken out. The Cook returns, unpaid by the regiment, and he instigates an argument between Mother Courage and the Chaplain. Yvette makes her second appearance, now a rich widow, much older and fatter, and reveals that the Cook was once her lover. Mother Courage leaves for the town, and Eilif is dragged along by soldiers. Again he has slaughtered some peasants and stolen their cattle, but it is now peacetime. He is executed for it, but his mother never finds out. She returns with the news that the war is back on again, and she now returns to business with the Cook in tow.

The seventeenth year of the war finds the world in a bleak condition, with nothing to trade and nothing to eat. The Cook inherits an inn in Utrecht and invites Mother Courage to run it with him, but he refuses to take Kattrin. Mother Courage is forced to turn him down, so the two go their separate ways. Pulling the wagon by themselves, Mother Courage and Kattrin hear an anonymous voice singing about the pleasure of having plenty.

The Catholics are besieging the Protestant town of Halle, and Mother Courage is away in the town, trading. Sleeping outside a peasant family's house, Kattrin is woken by their search party, who take one of the peasants with them as a guide. The peasant couple prays for the safety of those in the town, but Kattrin, unseen, gets a drum from the cart and climbs onto the roof. She beats the drum to try to awake the townspeople so that the siege can be anticipated. The soldiers return and shoot her, but before she dies, she is successful in awakening the town.

The next morning, Mother Courage sings a lullaby over her daughter's corpse, pays the peasants to bury her, and harnesses herself, alone, to the cart. The cart rolls back into action, but it is easier to pull now, since there is so little left in it to sell.

Summary and Analysis of Scene One

Mother Courage and Her Children opens with a recruiting officer and an army sergeant standing together, talking in the freezing snow. This nondescript picture is made specific only by a placard-heading announcement that the scene is in Dalecarlia. The recruiting officer complains bitterly about the difficulties of recruiting an army. Threatening suicide, he tells the sergeant that his difficulty finding honest, willing men to recruit has led to the loss of his faith in humanity. The sergeant explains, at length, that war is the only way of creating order.

To the sound of a jew's-harp, a covered cart rolls onto the stage. It is pulled by Mother Courage's two sons. Mother Courage is sitting aloft with Kattrin, her daughter, as she sings her opening song (note that in Brecht's 1949 production, the song was transposed to the very beginning of the play). The song advertises Mother Courage's wares to the army. Significantly, both verses of the song end with a chorus that describes whatever "has not died out / getting back to its feet again."

Mother Courage, unable to produce a valid set of papers, explains why she is called Courage (her real name is Anna Fierling): she once drove her cart through the bombardment of Riga in order to sell fifty molding loaves of bread. Mother Courage introduces her children (for the sake of exposition as much as for realistic detail) one by one. Eilif Nojocki is the son of a light-fingered soldier; Swiss Cheese, the son of a Swiss fortifications engineer; and Kattrin Haupt, half-German. Mother Courage immediately attempts to make a sale. The recruiting officer, however, is more interested in her son than the belt buckle she tries to sell him. Mother Courage reacts violently, pulling a knife and insisting that the soldiers keep away from her children.

An argument ensues between Mother Courage and the sergeant about the rights and wrongs of Eilif's signing up for service in the war. The sergeant points out that he has had a good life in the army, having joined at seventeen, but Mother Courage dryly comments that he is yet to reach seventy. Claiming a "second sight" which never reappears, Mother Courage then draws black crosses (signifying death) on slips of paper, and she invites the sergeant to select one. He is shaken when he draws a black cross. When Eilif seems keen to enlist, Mother Courage marks up several more black crosses and has each of her children draw one. She obviously has rigged the slips of paper, but in doing so she proves a prophet. All of her children are to die in the war, and Eilif is about to be taken from her under her nose.

Now distracting her by haggling over a belt buckle, the sergeant occupies Mother Courage while the recruiting officer leads Eilif off into the fields. Dumb Kattrin leaps from the cart, making hoarse noises, but Mother Courage is occupied with her trade and pays no heed. By the time she has pocketed her profits, her son is gone. "You"ll have to help pull now, Kattrin," Mother Courage says. Kattrin and Swiss Cheese, harnessed, pull the cart off into the distance as the sergeant speaks a final couplet:

If the war provides, then you

Have got to give it something too.

Analysis

Brecht opens his play with a conversation between two ordinary soldiers, the first of many choices emphasizing that this is a play about the war's effect on the little people. The setting is unglamorous, the soldiers are cold, and the issue they face is organizational and pragmatic. Rather than presenting an active battle, Brecht opens with a recruiting officer moaning about how difficult it is to get people involved in the war. Thus, the army is presented from the bottom up, rather than from the top down.

This first scene is also heavily ironic. That is, Brecht expects his audience to be alienated from the sergeant's hyperbolic stories about the villagers who forgot their names due to the absence of war, thus viewing the opening scene with a suitable degree of ironic detachment. The point is not that war really creates order, but that it is a system by which people and civilizations seem to survive--like capitalism with its markets, war is a system that most people not only accept but depend upon.

These nameless soldiers are universal, part of the trope of war's perpetuity, which runs throughout the play. In the 1949 production, the opening image of the cart revolving into view (actualy before the dialogue between the recruiting officer and the sergeant) was reflected at the end of the play when Mother Courage alone pulled it into the distance. War "gets back to its feet again," it continues, and Brecht is not interested in the specific historic details of the war he depicts. What he underlines is war's omnipresence in capitalist civilization.

The conflict between motherhood and business is immediately brought into focus by the cart. It is both home and a place of business. Mother Courage is distracted by business as Eilif is led away, and we see how her trade and her family life are irresolvably at odds: her interests as a mother and her interests as a businesswoman damage each other. Her children, fathered by a string of military men, might be thought of as "children of the war," and it is to the war that they will eventually succumb.

The flippancy with which Mother Courage cheats in making the black crosses ironically reflects her lack of awareness that the deaths she has predicted will indeed come to each of her children. The foreshadowing is not ominous so much as it is obvious: what Brecht wants us to realize is that Mother Courage does not see how she is tempting fate. She saves her children here only to lose one due to a business deal minutes later. Like the black crosses, her fate is in her own hands, but she does not realize this before having paid the price with Eilif.

There are more subtle foreshadowings in this scene. Mother Courage describes Eilif as so scared he'll "fall over like a chicken," and the recruiting officer adds, "and killing a young bull that happens to be in his way." For Eilif, who later will be commended and then executed for stealing cattle, this comment has an ominous resonance. Yet, even at this level, Brecht's larger themes are threaded into the narrative. Cattle, the spoils of war, are also the object of the market. By trying to feed himself, Eilif later feeds himself to the war. And like his mother's actions, his actions express a failure to see the larger picture. Probably, as the officers at the beginning of the scene seem to realize, the only way to be truly saved from the war is to refuse to participate in it in the first place--neither in its fighting nor in its business.

As in this scene, many scenes end with a character getting into the harness, ready to continue with the journey. At the end of Scene One, the yoke is heavy already.

Summary and Analysis of Scene Two

The scene heading announces that two years have passed and that Mother Courage is about to meet her son Eilif again. The stage is split in two, with on one side the General's tent and, on the other, his kitchen.

In the kitchen we meet General's cook (*der Koch*), to whom Mother Courage is attempting to sell a capon that she swindled from the peasants in the nearby village. After considerable bargaining, the Cook grudgingly buys the bird at the price of a florin. Mother Courage (along with the audience) is then privy to the scene in the parallel tent, where Eilif, a hero, is invited to dine with the General. He successfully killed some peasants and stolen the oxen they attempted to hide from the General's army. The General, absolutely delighted with Eilif's "heroic deed," pours him expensive wine. This luxury stands in stark contrast to the rotten beef and scrawny capon the Cook is preparing across the stage. The Chaplain, mocked by the General and with little to say about the scene's events, stands sullenly in the background.

Mother Courage, astonished to hear her son's voice again, comments that the General--being obsessed with the heroism of his troops--must be a very poor General. That is, if good battle strategies were in place, there would be no need for heroism.

Eilif sings the song of "The Girl and the Soldier," a grim parable about a soldier who dared to walk across frozen waters, not heeding the warnings of his "girl": he falls in, and, at the end of the song, disappears underneath. Mother Courage joins in with Eilif from the other side of the stage, and the two parties are united for the end of the scene. Mother Courage slaps her son around the face. She does so not, she explains, because he took the oxen, but because he put himself in danger. The scene finishes in the middle of this reprimand, with the General and the Chaplain ominously laughing in the doorway.

Analysis

"War as business idyll" was Brecht's summary of this scene in his summary of the dramaturgy. It is worth noting that, at this early stage of the play, the first military deed the play introduces us to is not really a military conquest but an illegal robbery carried out so that a hungry army could eat.

It is difficult to condemn Eilif for his deed insofar as he helped food go to hungry persons. As for the General, however, he is pompous, jingoistic, and living in luxury while his army eats "moldy bread." This figure of the war is at once ridiculous and morally corrupt. Brecht makes it very clear in his notes on the scene that the General should be played to demonstrate more than simply "rowdy drunkenness," and should display something of the absent obliviousness of the military aristocracy.

To fully understand its implications, one should read this scene in comparison with Scene Eight, where Eilif performs the same deed in peacetime and is executed for his trouble. What Brecht points out is not the criminality of war but the ways (as Scene One sets out) that war creates its own system of order. Eilif's heroic deed in wartime is a crime during peace.

Brecht's theatricality in this scene is also notable: the split stage is a crystal-clear attempt to force the audience to critically compare two realities by placing them literally side by side on the stage. Exactly what Brecht means his juxtaposition here to make us consider could be interpreted several ways: the Cook feeds the war with rotten meat in the kitchen, whereas Eilif "feeds" the war by stealing oxen on the other side of the stage. Mother Courage swindles peasants out of a capon on one side, whereas her son swindles peasants out of their oxen on the other. The basic juxtaposition is between the high-ranking levels of the army (the General is one of the highest-ranking military men to appear in the play) and the peasantry, while the innate capitalism of the war works upon every level of society.

Eilif's song, accompanied with a grotesquely carnivalesque "sword-dance," is a grisly irony .The repugnant celebration of his "peasant-slashing" and the joy taken in the horrific deeds of the war, juxtaposed with Mother Courage's plucking of the capon on the other side of the stage, reflect the surface message of the song itself. That is, the power of war is underestimated and seems to yield no clear winner.

Summary and Analysis of Scene Three

It is three years later. The cart is following a Finnish regiment, and a flagpole flies the regimental flag. The scene begins with another business transaction between Mother Courage and the war. She is trying to haggle down an armorer over the price of a sack of shot. "I'm not buying army goods,, she says at the beginning of the scene, before adding, "well, not at that price." She wins the bargaining and pays a florin and a half.

This is one of the play's more domestic scenes. Swiss Cheese, dressed in a paymaster's uniform, has fallen (like his brother) into the employ of the war. We are introduced to Yvette Pottier, an alcoholic prostitute who is drinking brandy, having set aside her red high-heels, and who sings the "Song of Fraternization" to warn Kattrin about the danger of getting involved with men. The song describes the relationship between Yvette and "Peter the Puff" (named thus because he kept his pipe in his mouth during sex) some years earlier, which culminated in Yvette being left behind as the regiment marched on. The play will later reveal "Peter the Puff" to be none other than the General's Cook. Depressed at the close of her song, Yvette exits, leaving her prostitute's garb behind her.

The Chaplain arrives with a message for Mother Courage from Eilif, and the Cook accompanies him (apparently to try his luck at a sexual relationship with Mother Courage). Mother Courage, the Cook and Chaplain discuss the politics of the war. The Kaiser is discussed in depth: he has followed his conscience but caused much bloodshed in doing what he believes is "the right thing." Mother Courage closes the conversation with the central observation that, though the big shots claim to be waging war for "Almighty God and all things bright and beautiful," they are actually "out for all they can get." During their conversation, Kattrin tries on Yvette's boots and hat and struts around, imitating Yvette.

There is a volley of gunfire, drumming, and explosions, and the armorer returns hurriedly to announce that the Catholics have taken over the regiment. A fast change of loyalty ensues with the Chaplain changing his robes and with Mother Courage changing the regimental flag, smearing Kattrin's face in ashes to make her less attractive to the invading soldiers. Swiss Cheese appears on the scene with the regimental cash box, and his mother is horrified to learn he wants to store it in her cart. The cannonfire intensifies, and there is a scene break.

Three days later, Swiss Cheese laments the fact he has not been able to return the cash box to his sergeant. Mother Courage leaves with the Chaplain to purchase meat (feeding the war again) after discovering Yvette's red high-heeled boots in the cart--Kattrin has stolen them during the Catholic raid.

While Swiss Cheese talks to Kattrin, a man with an eyepatch (a spy searching for Swiss Cheese) appears and asks her if she has seen anyone from the Second Finnish

Regimental Headquarters. Swiss Cheese, having decided to find his regiment and return the cashbox, ignores Kattrin's desperate attempts to warn him about the spy, takes the box, and leaves the scene.

As Mother Courage arrives back with the Chaplain, Swiss Cheese is dragged back on by two men and questioned about a sergeant--he hid the cashbox by the river, was followed, and was caught. His mother denies knowing him, and he is led off. There is another scene break.

The Chaplain sings to Kattrin the "song of the Hours," which outlines the Passion of Christ in brief quatrains. Yvette enters with an ancient colonel with whom she is sleeping. She haggles with Mother Courage about buying her cart. Mother Courage is forced to agree since she needs money to bribe the soldiers to spare Swiss Cheese's life. Yvette runs offstage to persuade the soldiers to take the bribe.

Mother Courage intends to use the money from the cashbox to buy her cart back from Yvette once Swiss Cheese has returned. As her plan goes, Swiss Cheese will turn over the cashbox to her. Yet, when Yvette returns, it is to tell her that the soldiers will accept her two hundred florins as a bribe--but that Swiss Cheese, under torture, admitted to throwing the cashbox in the river. Mother Courage now has to choose between her business and her son.

She tells Yvette to return offering one hundred twenty florins, so that she has some money left over with which to continue trading. The soldiers refuse, demanding the full two hundred and refusing to wait. Yvette runs back to offer the full amount, but it is too late. Drums are heard in the distance, and the stage lights darken. Swiss Cheese has been executed.

The soldiers return with Swiss Cheese's body on a stretcher. To save herself and her daughter, Mother Courage again denies knowing him, shaking her head in silence. The sergeant commands his men to throw Swiss Cheese's corpse into the pit since "there ain't nobody here who knows him."

Analysis

As well as being the longest scene, this is one of the key scenes in the play, deserving serious attention. It combines several of the play's key themes and is perhaps the easiest scene to analyze in terms of Brecht's use of dramatic symbolism.

Family vs. business, an irresolvable conflict which is to cost Swiss Cheese his life at the end of the scene, expresses tensions from the start: Mother Courage's washing line is strung from a cannon, a visual symbol of the way Mother Courage's domestic and professional lives are always inextricably linked. Brecht's message is neatly underlined too in the way that Mother Courage attempts to "mortgage," not "sell," her cart to Yvette. But like her own involvement in the war, this bargain too must be an all-or-nothing deal. Even the cart itself, home and business, is caught somewhere between these two poles.

Mother Courage's bargaining for Swiss Cheese's life was much edited by Brecht after the original premiere of the play in order to make Mother Courage seem less sympathetic. From the final text of the play, it is easy to condemn her for, as she herself puts it, "bargaining too long" and thereby bringing about her son's shooting. The paradox here is that Mother Courage herself will starve if she retains no means by which to live--the sale of her cart represents financial ruin for her. Though it is easy to refute, in retrospect, Mother Courage's decision to bargain, Brecht emphasizes that often, for the peasant classes, the choice is often between one dire circumstance and another.

Mother Courage's bargaining highlights what Brecht said was the single most important lesson of the play as a whole: that little people cannot profit from a war which runs only for the profit of the greater authorities. Mother Courage here fails to realize that she will never be able to save Swiss Cheese and keep her cart. There is an opportunity cost either way. According to Brecht, Mother Courage's greatest failing is that although a capitalist, even at the end of the play she remains ignorant of this basic truth about capitalism. (See the section on "Brecht's Intention.")

This scene is also fascinating in terms of its religious symbolism. As well as being the third scene in the play, occurring three years after the second scene, one of its central breaks is for three days. These recurring threes culminate in Mother Courage's denying knowing Swiss Cheese three times. And once we hear the Chaplain's "Song of the Hours," it is hard for anyone with a good education to miss Brecht's comparison of Swiss Cheese's death with the Passion of Jesus. Yet the sergeant's final instruction, to "throw Swiss Cheese in the pit," suggests that Swiss Cheese is no martyr who has died for a good cause. The comparison goes the other way: invoking the suffering and death of Jesus in this way sidelines, in the context of war, the role of religion. The Passion is likened to a minor military execution outside a tiny village--an insignificant act, achieving nothing.

The rejection of a role for religious belief among wartime capitalists is explicit in the scene's action as well. The Chaplain's hypocrisy is clear as day in his bitter line, "All good Catholics here," and it seems not to matter to Mother Courage which religion's flag she flies. The speed with which the Chaplain changes his robes when he learns the Catholics are attacking demonstrates that his religious principles are instantly superseded by his cowardice in the face of danger. At the same time, one might think that the differences between Protestants and Catholics are not so great after all, making it easier for people to switch allegiances for non-religious reasons. "Bribery in humans is like mercy in God," says Mother Courage at one point, and the provocation of this comparison is only one of many points where Brecht forces us to question the value of religious faith in what is, after all, supposed to be a war of religion.

One of Brecht's single most famous pieces of direction, the "silent scream," was included in the first production at the very end of the scene after Swiss Cheese's body is carried away. Helene Weigel, playing Mother Courage, screamed silently. Brecht wrote, "her look of extreme suffering after she has heard the shots, her unscreaming open mouth and backward-bent head probably derived from a press photograph of an Indian woman crouched over the dead body of her son during the shelling of Singapore." Its resonance has indeed proved powerfully timeless, and it is retained in many modern productions (including Stephen Unwin's 2006 ETT staging, which starred Diana Quick). Perhaps it is so powerful because, like Mother Courage herself at that moment, it is painfully ineffective yet intensely personal. A "silent scream" is a paradox understood best by the screamer.

Kattrin's character comes into interesting focus within the spectrum of sexual undercurrents in the relationships in this scene. The Cook, by leaving his pipe (already noted as a sexual symbol by Yvette earlier) with Mother Courage, has thereby declared his sexual interest in her. Yet, though her mother remains sexually desirable, Kattrin's imitation of Yvette's gait and theft of her prostitute's boots is a telling representation of the way her mother represses Kattrin's own burgeoning sexuality. Kattrin's awakening desires in the scene will be another, more subtle, victim of the war.

Summary and Analysis of Scene Four

Mother Courage is discovered waiting outside the captain's tent, intending to complain about the ransacking of her cart. His clerk advises her not to bother complaining.

A young soldier, led by an old soldier, enters--aggressive, swearing, and furiously attempting to make his own complaint. He complains that the captain himself has kept the prize money which he won by swimming the river.

Mother Courage sings to him the "Song of the Great Capitulation." It details the way she, when she was young, had high ideals and aspirations but now, like everyone does, has succumbed to marching in step with the band--a metaphor for willingly participating in the war.

After she has finished the song, Mother Courage advises the young soldier to stick out the wait and complain, but only if his anger is "big enough" to be able to resist such a capitulation. The young soldier shouts, "lick my arse!" and exits.

The clerk pops his head back out of the captain's tent and tells Mother Courage that the captain is now ready to hear her complaint. She tells him she no longer wants to complain.

Analysis

When the young soldier is led by an old soldier, we see this scene's key theme: the passing on of wisdom from the old to the young. Note the reflection of Achilles' anger against Agamemnon (from the Iliad in the young soldier's anger that the captain took the prize that justly belongs to the soldier.

That this scene is considerably shorter than some of the plot-driven scenes in this play points to the scene's function as a parable within the play. The ransacking of Mother Courage's cart is never revisited or even mentioned again. The scene mainly shows Courage capitulating by losing the will to complain. War, in short, crushes the will. "This scene," wrote Brecht, "calls for bitterness at the start and dejection at the end." Thus is the progression of Mother Courage, yet at the play's close, the song's lyrics are recalled when Mother Courage really does march literally "in step with the band" as she makes her final exit.

We might have expected her to mourn for the son she has lost as a result of the Catholic incursion, yet she is more actively concerned with the loss of her trade. And, though Brecht called the song "bitter," he went further in condemning Mother Courage's actions: "in no scene is Courage as depraved as in this one."

This depravity is not, as many interpreters have it, because Courage is advocating capitulation, but because she is blessed in this scene with a rare self-awareness: she knows that her complaining is worthless unless it has the power to result in a change. It is not that Courage should not rock the boat, but rather that there is no point in complaining *unless* the boat is rocked. She sees the light here, and what Brecht condemns is that she does not act upon it. Sadly, she is condemned in her resignation to the idea that at her level nothing can be done.

Summary and Analysis of Scene Five

Two years later, Mother Courage's cart has stopped in a badly shot-up village--during Tilly's victory at Leipzig (1631). Courage refuses to give a soldier a drink because he cannot pay. The soldier has a fur coat slung over his shoulder, which he has looted from the village.

The Chaplain stumbles on, asking urgently for bandages and linen. He carries in the mother of a peasant's family. They have refused to abandon their farm even during heavy gunfire. Courage tells him she has no bandages and refuses to help.

When the Chaplain asks again and is greeted with blind refusals from Courage, Kattrin attempts to threaten her mother with a plank of wood. Eventually, by lifting her off the steps of the cart, the Chaplain forcefully takes four of Courage's officer's shirts, tearing them into strips to use as bandages.

From the house comes "the pained cry of a child." Kattrin rushes into the fray to rescue a baby, which she brings back into the scene, rocking it in her arms. Courage laments the loss of her expensive shirts and then pounces on the soldier (from the start of the scene) for attempting to steal schnapps. She snatches the looted fur coat from his shoulders.

Analysis

Tilly's sacking of Magdeburg was one of the bloodiest atrocities of the Thirty Years' War. It was unparalleled in the number of civilian casualties. The grimly ironic final sentence of the scene heading tells us that the sacking "costs Mother Courage four officers' shirts." As in Scene Two, the startling comparison forces the audience to critically examine the action. Can the cost to Courage really ever be equated with the lives lost? The paradoxical answer is that, for Courage, everything has a price and can be compared. Besides, Courage's trade--and these shirts in particular--represent her own survival. To make allowances, as she rightly points out, might mean to starve.

This is one of the most revised scenes in the play. Brecht originally had had Courage tear up some of the shirts into bandages herself, but after the unsatisfactory premiere he rewrote the scene to make Courage seem still less sympathetic. In the scene as we have it now, Courage makes no concessions to necessity as far as her officers' shirts are concerned, yielding a far less compassionate portrayal than was originally intended.

This is also a key scene for Kattrin and her relationship with her mother. Her spontaneous (and deeply felt) attempted assault ties into the way she recklessly risks her own life to save the baby later. Whereas Courage always can put her business sense above her heart, her daughter, it appears, never can. In the original production, at the end of this scene, Courage held high her fur coat on one side of the stage, while Kattrin held high her baby on the other. The contrast between the two priorities (and the two acquisitions) is illuminating and paves the way for Kattrin's death (and Courage's life) at the end of the play. Note whose values win in the end--which might be more a statement of tragedy than of poetic justice.

Summary and Analysis of Scene Six

Mother Courage is enjoying a newfound prosperity, and she undertakes a stock check on the day of the funeral of the fallen general Tilly. She refuses to allow some low-ranking soldiers into her tent, but she happily sells them brandy--they have dodged out of the funeral. Courage feels sorry for the dead general, lamenting the way the common people do not lend their full support to the larger plans.

There is then a long conversation about the duration of the war, with Mother Courage anxiously raising the crucial question of how long it will last. If it is to continue, she can comfortably invest in new goods for the cart. If it will finish soon, she cannot risk investing for fear of being left with unsaleable goods. The Chaplain convinces her that the war will last--there might be a short hiatus, but war always will ultimately continue. The Clerk wants peace to come, but the Chaplain thinks that the Pope and Emperor will contrive to keep the soldiers fighting. Comparing it to love, he seems to see war's continuance as a positive thing. Talking of the redundancy of peace in today's climate, he poses the riddling phrase, "what is the hole once the cheese is eaten?"

Kattrin runs angrily behind the cart at the Chaplain's verdict (her mother has insisted she wait until peacetime before she gets a male friend). She is sent immediately to pick up some merchandise from a nearby camp. "Don't let them take anything" says Courage, and again, playing on her daughter's sexual repression for the good of her business, "think of your dowry."

After Kattrin has left, Courage lights up the Cook's pipe, and the Chaplain converses with her as he chops firewood. He dislikes the Cook, while Courage quite likes him, a foreshadowing of their future sexual partnership. He complains that his clerical talents are being underused, and--with ambiguous motives--suggests a marriage, or at least a closer (perhaps sexual) relationship. She hints that she does not want to take anyone into her business, and when he tries to appeal to her soul, she tells him, "I don't have a soul. I do, however, need firewood." All she wants, she says in this scene, is to "get my kids through this war" (a goal, we will see, that will never be achieved).

Kattrin staggers back in, having been assaulted while bringing the merchandise back to her mother. But she has not, significantly, dropped or disregarded any of the merchandise she was supposed to be carrying. Courage dresses her wound and attempts to comfort her by presenting her with Yvette's red shoes, hidden in the cart. Kattrin rejects them and crawls back into the cart. Courage, examining the merchandise with which Kattrin has returned with, and for the only time in the play, curses the war.

Analysis

Like the fighting, the big event of the war--Tilly's funeral--happens offstage. Again, Brecht keeps the focus on the little people rather than the world-level leaders. The possibility of peace hangs over the scene. Peace actually will ruin Courage's business, but it will delight her daughter. The audience's sympathy, and the moral high ground, is clearly with Kattrin's sexual desires rather than her mother's financial ones.

Yet, the scene brutally cauterizes Kattrin's ambiguous sexual awakening with a brutal attack. Shortly before she goes on her mother's errand, Kattrin's hopes of acquiring a husband are dashed by the Chaplain's forecast of a perpetual war. The scar on her face as a result of the assault will prevent her from ever attaining a husband. This is what Courage suggests, and her idea is supported by the events of the play.

The reason Kattrin rejects the red boots at the end of the scene is not because she is morally superior to the sexual promiscuity that they represent (Yvette, their previous owner, is a prostitute) but because they are no longer of any use. Disfigured, she will never know the joys of a marriage bed, and she will never have the children of her own that she so clearly desires.

The scene's focus on marriage also extends into an unflattering insight into the Chaplain. Watching her smoke the pipe (smoked during intercourse by Yvette's "Peter the Puff") incites a desire for her body and her business. She rejects him in terms of the business. The only attractive morals in this scene are Kattrin's, though the literal disfiguration that the war gives her in this scene destroys the possibility of these morals taking root beyond Kattrin. The role of Kattrin's dumbness is thus neatly underlined.

Summary and Analysis of Scene Seven

Business is good. The cart is pulled by Kattrin and the Chaplain (or the "chaplain-potboy," as Brecht has it in his model). Courage sings to the audience cheerily, advertising her wares. She praises the war as a good provider.

Analysis

This very brief scene represents the brevity of good fortunes in times of war. Nevertheless, Mother Courage is "at the height of her business career," appearing to get something good out of the war. No longer is she cursing the war or regretting the pressure it puts on her and her family; no longer does she seem to have as her only desire to "get with my kids, through this war." This momentary prosperity has distracted her from the death of Swiss Cheese, the assault of Kattrin, and the loss of Eilif.

"If there's a war on, I'll get involved," she declares at the end of the song. This is further approval of the capitalist system. In the original production, Brecht had Weigel wearing a necklace of silver talers and rings on her fingers--these, he wrote, show her up for what she is, bribed.

Her claim that the weak lose during times of peace as well as times of war reiterates the Chaplain's argument that peace is simply war undeclared. Capitalism reigns, and as Brecht unrelentingly shows us, the only escape is to opt out altogether. (The alternative is not really given, although the peasants seem to live their lives under some kind of alternative.) In this scene, Courage quite openly opts in.

Summary and Analysis of Scene Eight

Waking her from her sleep in the cart, two nameless peasants, an old woman and her son, attempt to sell Mother Courage their father's bedding. They need to get the money because they are so hungry.

Bells begin to ring and voices shout that the Swedish king has been killed--and as a result, peace has broken out. Some Lutherans have ridden into town and brought the news with them. The old woman faints in shock at the news, and her son picks her up, heading for home with the tragicomic line, "Dad'll get his bed back."

The Cook appears, "somewhat bedraggled," having not been paid by the army and therefore wandering unemployed and hungry in search of food. As Scene Two suggested, he has been blamed for the lack of food that has spread across the country. Thus, in line with his name, he has become a sacrificial lamb. His high spirits have been somewhat dampened by the last eight years of war. The Chaplain, on hearing of the peace, changes back into his clerical robes.

The Cook and Courage discuss her decision to buy more wares. Now that peace has broken out, it looks like she will be ruined. The Cook blames the Chaplain for making a bad decision. When the Chaplain returns, now in his robes, an argument ensues during which the Chaplain loses his temper with Courage, blaspheming against peace and calling her a "hyena of the battlefield." He tells her, "you only want war, not peace, because you make a profit from it: in which case you should never forget that he who sups with the devil needs a long spoon."

Courage then tells him that they must go their separate ways. The Cook advises her to get to market to sell her wares, and she immediately gets ready to leave.

Yvette appears, "much older and fatter and heavily powdered," followed by a servant. She married the brother of the Colonel she was with in Scene Three, and she inherited a fortune on his death. She recognizes the Cook as "Peter the Puff" and now stresses her status against him, treating him as a commoner in light of her new noble status. Courage goes off to market with Yvette.

The Chaplain and the Cook have a short conversation. Eilif is brought on, chalk-white and escorted by soldiers with pikes. He is here to see his mother, and he has been arrested for breaking into a peasants' farm. It is exactly the deed he committed in wartime, but it has become a crime when committed during peacetime. Eilif is taken away to be shot, the Chaplain following at his heels.

Courage returns with the news that peacetime is over after all. The Lutherans are involved in a shooting match with the townspeople. As Kattrin and the Cook harness themselves up, Courage sings another business song.

Analysis

Peace is short-lived. The Chaplain seems to be correct to say that peace is just a hiatus between wars. By the time the news of peace travels to the town, it is about time for the peace to be over.

Courage has quite literally bought into the capitalist system of war. She still needs the war to be able to recoup her investment. She keeps to this system despite the fact that, under her nose in the same scene, the war also kills her son.

Eilif's death establishes in the audience's mind that, true to the inevitability of an Aristotelian tragedy, all of Courage's children are to be lost to the war. Kattrin's death now seems only a matter of when: it seems clear now that it will happen. What remains to be seen is whether or not Courage will realize tragically that her own involvement in the war as a business empire is something conducive to the desolation of her family. But the shattering anticlimax of the ending is that she never does. Brecht gives the audience a chance to see and consider this tragic situation ourselves, not distracted by either silent or loud screams.

It is no accident that, even at the very end of the play, Eilif's death remains unknown to Mother Courage. She is trading at the market when it happens. As with Swiss Cheese's death in Scene Three, and like Kattrin's coming death in Scene Eleven, her business distracts her from her family.

The Chaplain's final scene has him launch a rather hypocritical attack on Courage, a failed attempt to take the moral high ground on the premise that she hopes for war rather than peace. His exit with Eilif is unusually anticlimactic. For one of the play's central characters, his story is brought to no real resolution, only an abrupt ending. He has made little difference in the play itself, but he has been exposed repeatedly as a self-seeking hypocrite and turncoat rather than a morally driven man of the cloth. Yet, before he exits, the short conversation between him and the Cook about cabbage and carrots foreshadows Beckett's Waiting for Godot in its representation of the poignant misery that war brings to the human heart. Here is another facet of Brecht's focus on heartbreakingly small details rather than the bigger picture.

The other key entrance in this scene is that of Yvette, who is the only person in the play who profits from the war. She has paid for it with her beauty, needing to wait for an inheritance to find her profit. She is fatter and much older, implying that she has aged past her years. "She has sold herself," Brecht writes in the model, "but for a good price." And, of course, what she really wanted, the love of the Cook or "Peter the Puff," is now farther away than ever. She expresses a genuine bitterness in the way she chastizes him as a commoner. What might have been supposed a recognition or *anagnorisis* is in fact a non-event: the young, attractive Yvette whom Peter once loved has been traded in the market of the war.

Summary and Analysis of Scene Nine

It is the seventeenth year of "the great war of faith," a "grey morning in early winter." Mother Courage and the Cook, dressed in shabby sheepskins, draw the cart. They stop outside a small house, belonging presumably to a parson. They intend to beg for food; they are starving and cold.

The Cook reveals to Courage that he has received a letter from his aunt in Utrecht, telling him that his mother has died and that he has inherited the family inn. He invites Mother Courage to come with him and run the inn. After so many years of war, they are both tired, and as Courage sees, people are desperately poor, having nothing to buy her wares with. "Nothing's growing, except brambles."

She immediately tells Kattrin of the Cook's offer--but he pulls her aside and makes it clear that there is no room at the inn for Kattrin to live as well. If Courage is to accept his offer, Kattrin must remain behind. She will, the Cook thinks, never find a husband with that scar, so she might as well continue to pull the cart. Courage considers.

Mother Courage and the Cook then sing the "Song of Solomon" outside the parson's house as they beg for food and charity. The song details the way that great virtues do little to save great men from great disaster--examining, in order, Solomon, Julius Caesar, Socrates, and Saint Martin. It closes with a verse that deals with the "respectable folk" who are singing the song. At the close of the song, a voice calls Courage and the Cook into the parsonage for hot soup, and they go in. Courage then refuses to leave her daughter. The Cook accepts her decision with cool logic.

Kattrin, who has overheard much of the conversation about the Inn in Utrecht, emerges with a bundle, intending to run away. She lays out a pair of the cook's trousers and lays them on top of an old skirt of her mother's, but she is caught in the act by her mother. Guiltily, Mother Courage comforts Kattrin, and throwing the Cook's stuff out of the cart, the two of them get back on the road together. When the Cook arrives out of the parsonage with his soup, he looks bleakly at his possessions.

Analysis

By this late stage in the play, the glorious prosperity celebrated in Scene Seven has been lost. Times are hard, the weather is cold, and there is little business for Courage. The little people, in this scene, really cannot make any cut from the war. Nothing is growing, and there is nothing to buy or sell. The brutal message of the play about the war's ravages is now explicit.

Brecht is also moving towards the resolution of the play's plot. When Courage and the Cook have their brutal conversation about Kattrin's chances of marriage, having Kattrin overhear them makes her deeply and immediately sympathetic. Rejected and dejected, Kattrin "decides to spare her mother the need to make a decision" (*Couragemodell*) and leaves a message, the trousers and skirts, to accuse her mother of being a whore to the war. Courage's lies and comforting do little to lift the uncomfortable resonance of Kattrin's pictorial accusation--both Kattrin and the audience know that Courage was seriously considering the Cook's offer and that her protestations to the contrary are simply lies.

It is important, Brecht wrote, not to represent the Cook as "brutal" in this scene. The fact is that the tavern he has inherited is too small and, of course, the customers cannot be expected to put up with the sight of the disfigured Kattrin. The logic applied is such as might be expected in a business proposition. Here in abundance are the lack of humanity and the lack of compassion that characterize the dealings of the war.

This is the Cook's final scene. Like the Chaplain's in Scene 8, it is another minor exit for a major character. Ernst Busch, the Cook after 1951 in Brecht's production, indicated the sexual nature of this parting of ways by letting his pipe first droop and then fall from his mouth. And, though he has been absent from much of the play, the Cook is notably the play's most humorous character. His blank, silent exit, with his few belongings lying in front of him on an open stage, is a notable sign that there are to be no more laughs. Brecht's play is now moving towards its brutal, unforgiving, pessimistic conclusion.

Summary and Analysis of Scene Ten

The scene heading announces that during the year 1635, Mother Courage and Kattrin travel over the high roads of central Germany. As they pull the cart, they pass a peasant's house, out of which a voice sings a song with two short verses. The first describes a garden with roses in it. The voice rather smugly talks of how happy are people with gardens because they can see the lovely flowers. The second describes the coldness of winter before concluding that those with a thatched roof are happy since they have shelter from the cold. Mother Courage and Kattrin pause to listen and then pull the cart off.

Analysis

As in Scene Five, this scene serves more as a parable than as a direct part of the plot. "The Song of Home" was sung in Brecht's original production with "unfeeling, provocative self-assurance. The arrogant pride of possession expressed in the singing turned the listeners on the road into damned souls." It is a momentary, almost grotesque glimpse (which might be compared to that of the General in Scene Two) of life on the other side-this is the attitude of the people who, despite the war, are above the bread line. The audience may be repulsed to hear these words while seeing the poverty personified in Courage and Kattrin. Yet, it is significant that Mother Courage and Kattrin say absolutely nothing. What is going through their minds is left to the imagination. Peter Thomson makes the fascinating observation that "one [or both?] of them is surely thinking of an inn in Utrecht" (See *Plays in Production: Mother Courage and her Children.*)

Summary and Analysis of Scene Eleven

It is January 1636. The emperor's troops are threatening the Protestant town of Halle, and the cart stands, much the worse for wear, alongside a peasant's house with a huge thatched roof. It is the middle of the night.

An ensign and three soldiers in heavy armor come out of the wood and drag out a peasant, his son, and his wife. Kattrin is dragged out of the cart. Mother Courage has again, we are told, gone into town to trade. The soldiers need to find a guide to take them into the town in order to besiege it. When they threaten the peasants' oxen, the son agrees and leads them off into the town.

The peasant and his wife conclude that there is nothing to be done to wake up the sleeping people in the town without risking their own lives. With Kattrin, they kneel to pray for God's mercy. Kattrin begins to groan as the peasant's wife, leading the prayer, mentions the "four children of my brother-in-law," who are asleep in their house in the town. When she notes that one child is "not yet two, and the eldest seven," Kattrin stands up, unseen. She takes a drum from the cart, climbs onto the roof, and begins to beat the drum to awaken the sleeping townspeople.

The peasants desperately try to get her to come down. Kattrin pulls the ladder up onto the roof. They threaten to throw stones at her, terrified that the soldiers will return and murder them. The soldiers return and attempt to get her down. They try to muffle the noise of the drum by chopping trees with an axe. They threaten her with the death of her mother and try to smash up the cart. But Kattrin keeps drumming. Eventually they fetch a harquebus and shoot Kattrin, who "slowly crumples," beats the drum a few more times, and then falls dead.

Yet, as Kattrin's body slumps, cannon fire and confused noises are heard from the town. She has succeeded in awaking the townsfolk, though she has given her own life in doing so.

Analysis

This scene is one of the most dramatic in the play. It was criticized by many of Brecht's contemporaries for being more of the "Dramatic Theater" than of the "Epic Theater." It is indeed a danger of the scene that the dynamism and excitement of its events might prevent the audience from critically viewing it. Yet, Brecht's point is to illustrate the importance of acting versus not action. He noted that it was essential that the peasants' justification of their failure to act must be presented so as to make it obvious that prayer is the final point in a line of argument which justifies their "not acting." Kattrin, in contrast, is not praying but is taking matters into her own hands. Her action is praised while religion is demeaned in this period of wartime.

The scene heading contains the strangely figurative line, "The stone speaks." The "stone" must be Kattrin (influenced, perhaps, by Shakespeare's line "dumb breathing stones" in *Richard III*, or by the Biblical idea of the stones crying out for justice). Thus, her actions in this scene might be considered the most eloquent in the play. It is highly ironic that it is by making noise that the silent (dumb) Kattrin finally achieves this eloquence. She has been silent throughout the play, yet it is the sound she creates now that will save lives. Kattrin sacrifices herself to save a town of people. Whether or not she is successful, we are never told, but Brecht clearly intends the attempt to be seen as noble.

Nevertheless, criticism is divided on the issue of Kattrin's sainthood. Many commentators have suggested that she only takes action because of the mention of the children who will die in the siege. If Kattrin is obsessed with babies and childhood, does this make her deed less noble? That is, how aware is she of the magnitude of her deed-is she doing it for the whole town or just for the children? These questions make for interesting discussion when analyzing Kattrin's character. Even so, in the spectrum of main characters in this play, Kattrin's actions here make her character the most praiseworthy. She gives her own life for a noble cause.

Kattrin's death represents the emotional climax of the play. It is the death of Courage's final child and the culmination of the play's growing focus on Kattrin's character. At the same time, the high drama of the scene becomes almost comedic: the soldiers are presented as fatally stupid, and their attempts to drown out Kattrin's drumming by chopping wood are risible-they just add noise that will awaken the town. Symbolically, is Kattrin a tree that needs to be chopped down in this time of war?

Summary and Analysis of Scene Twelve

Mother Courage sings a lullaby over Kattrin's dead body. It is time for her to get back on the road. The peasants advise her to follow the regiment immediately. Fetching a tarpaulin from her cart, she covers Kattrin's body. She pays the peasants to bury her. Mother Courage harnesses herself to the cart, hoping that she can pull it alone. The noise of a regiment passes by, and Courage follows along with it, pulling the cart. From offstage, the song that introduced Courage in Scene One is repeated to end the play.

Analysis

The lullaby, according to Brecht, was to be sung "without any sentimentality or desire to provoke sentimentality." Its innate materialism must be made clear. The lullaby itself sets the extraordinary prosperity of a child in competition with that of other children. *This* child, Courage's child, must be the best. Even in mourning her last child, Courage is unable to separate herself from the cut-and-thrust of the competitive capitalist market. Courage's way of life, even her means of discourse, is her trade. To illustrate this point, which has become rather obvious by this scene, many productions have adopted Brecht's choice in the original production whereby Courage, in paying the peasants for Kattrin's burial, extracts three coins from her purse, but hands over only two, putting one back.

Weigel's portrayal of Courage in the original production made her seem eighty years old in this scene, according to Brecht. The war has wearied her, her business is depleted by it, and her children (though she still does not know about Eilif) have all been killed at its hands. Yet, she has learned nothing. She and her cart will continue. The final line she speaks is, "I've got to get back into business." She has not learned Brecht's lesson that "those who will make their cut from the war need a very big pair of scissors." In this play, war is a capitalist system that makes the rich richer and the poor poorer.

This scene can be a stumbling block for actors who play Courage. If they get involved in the scene rather than maintaining their consistent "attitude" toward it (a basic premise of Brecht's "epic" acting style), the audience will leave the theater with the impression that this indefatigable woman has endured the worst and has still come through, that is, her aim of "coming through the war" has been achieved. But this is not at all what Brecht desired, and this interpretation would undermine the play's aim as a whole. Remember that peace is fleeting. If Mother Courage represents a system that is problematic by nature, it makes sense that she does not change her nature despite all of the problems she faces. One reconciles oneself to the war and to what one finds in the world; if one wants to change it, one needs a very big mechanism for change.

The final image of the play reiterates the words of the song that accompanies it and which began the play. As the Chaplain suggested, war does not die, but rests; what is not yet dead gets back onto its feet for the next round. The cart's rolling around the stage (often accomplished in modern productions using a revolve) represents the perpetuity of war. From the play's setting in the Thirty Years' War to its composition during the Second World War (and to our own time), we remain war-torn and in need of Brecht's timeless lessons.

Suggested Essay Questions

1. **How good a mother is Mother Courage? How courageous is she?**

   This question asks you to consider what counts as a "good mother" and what counts as "courage"--both as presented in the play and as what seems true to you. In thinking about Courage in these terms, consider her attitude towards her children when there is a conflict of interest with her business.
2. **"All good Catholics here" (Chaplain, Scene 3). What is the role of religion within the religious war in which the play is set?**

   The quotation is a clue that the Chaplain is the key character to analyze in answering this question. One good answer would attempt a character study of him before relating it outward to the bigger pictures of the war and the play.
3. **Explore Brecht's presentation of Kattrin, commenting particularly on the significance of her being dumb (mute).**

   Writing about Kattrin can be difficult in that she speaks no lines. Consider, though, moments where Brecht gives her specific gestures in the stage directions, and analyze her growing role in the play, particularly her final scene. Consider also what other characters say about her and whether we should believe what they say, and how others react to her character.
4. **Is *Mother Courage and Her Children* a tragedy?**

   Remember to define tragedy before relating that definition to the play. See the section on Major Themes for help.
5. **Using your knowledge of Brecht's "epic theater," comment on the songs and their role within the play.**

   There are twelve songs in the play, so choose the ones that are most relevant to your thesis. See the glossary for key terms, and consider the songs' effects on the audience with respect to both thought and emotion.
6. **Brecht claimed that his first intention was to force his audience to critically analyze his characters and their decisions--the audience's emotional involvement was not nearly as important. Does this play achieve that goal?**

   Consider your own emotional response to the play, particularly in your first experience of it. For most readers the response will be based around the final two scenes. Decide whether or not it is possible to critically analyze them while watching the scenes or thinking about them using one's memory. Good answers might consider the possibility that different productions of the play can have different levels of success.
7. **Write a character study of the Cook, commenting on the way he ties**

into the theme of "feeding the war."

See the other sections of this ClassicNote for pointers about the Cook and this theme. Note who the Cook spends his time with, what he says, and what characters expect him to be and do.

8. **Do you agree with critics who argue that Brecht's scene headings and placards give too much away, making each scene predictable or boring?**

   Here, it will help to relate your knowledge of Brecht's theater choices and practices to your own view of how the play can work as a whole. What happens in some of the scenes that cannot be captured in the headings and notes? Also see the section on Brecht and Epic Theater.

9. **Brecht wrote, "Yvette Pottier is the only character in the play who strikes it rich; she has sold herself for a good price." Examine Yvette's character in light of this assertion.**

   Yvette is the most interesting character to analyze in examining the theme of class, so a good answer might include some discussion of class. Consider too how Yvette, like Courage, sacrifices her emotional needs for financial ones. And what do you make of the idea of selling oneself? Is that ever morally acceptable?

10. **Brecht wrote, "I am curious to know how many of those who see *Mother Courage and Her Children* today understand its warning" (Brecht "Theaterarbeit," 1952). What do you understand to be the play's warning?**

    See the additional content on "Brecht's Intention" for an analysis of what Brecht thought the answer to this question was. Does this warning make sense in light of your own reading of the play? Consider how far the play is still relevant in your time and place.

11. **Brecht called his play a "Chronicle of the Thirty Years' War." How far does the title "Chronicle" fit the play and the playwright's intentions?**

    (Look up "Chronicle" in a dictionary if necessary.) This question relates to the play as a whole and how it might affect an audience. Consider what a chronicle or another kind of history is supposed to achieve. Is that what Brecht achieves?

12. **Relate Brecht's play to the "dark times" in which it was written. How far do you find Brecht's setting of the Thirty Years' War relevant to the times in which he lived?**

    This question asks for knowledge of the two contexts of Brecht's play: the time when it was written, and the time when it was set. These contexts then have to be related to each other. There is a small amount of information about both on this site, but the key is to consider which lessons Brecht thought he learned from the Thirty Years' War as portrayed in the play, and then to learn enough history to assess whether those lessons actually can be drawn reasonably from both the Thirty Years' War and from Brecht's own time.

About "Epic Theater"

Brecht felt strongly about the generally apolitical nature of the theater around which he grew up, particularly the realistic drama of Konstantin Stanislavski. When he began working as a writer and a director, the Second World War was looming large on the horizon, and Brecht believed that theater should engage more directly with the political climate of its day.

"Epic Theater" was Brecht's term for the form of theater he hoped would achieve this goal. Its basic aim was to educate its audience by forcing them to view the action of the play critically, from a detached, "alienated," point of view, rather than allow them to become emotionally involved. Coleridge's famous "willing suspension of disbelief," where the audience switched off its critical faculties in order to believe in the world of the play, had met its polar opposite.

Though his work was not always successful in this aim, Brecht devised several very famous techniques through which he could achieve a high level of critical detachment. These included placards that summarized the plot of the scene before the scene itself was played out. This technique decreases anticipation and tension, and it renders the plot inevitable. The songs were sung half in character and half out of character, which helps to comment dryly on the events of the play. The sets were spare and cold, using a minimum of stage furniture. In these circumstances, the audience can focus more easily on why the events happen and on what message is being conveyed.

It also is significant that Brecht asked his actors to play his characters with a permanent degree of critical awareness. He wanted an attitude *to* rather than an immersion *in* the character being played, and he demanded that the actors--as well he might, considering that plays like Mother Courage and Her Children include songs--be constantly aware of how they were playing their parts. Not only that, but Brecht also asked his actors to make clear that one choice was being made in favor to another. He often wrote dialogue accordingly. See, for example, the peasants' justification of their failure to act in Scene Eleven of Mother Courage and Her Children.

The purpose of the theater thus was not to imitate life but to educate the audience. Brecht wrote that there was "no more noble aim for any theater."

Brecht's Intention

Mother Courage and Her Children, Brecht wrote, should teach the audience the lesson Courage herself fails to learn at the end of the play. In Brecht's own words:

> *What is a performance of Mother Courage and Her Children primarily intended to show?*
>
> That in wartime the big profits are not made by little people. That war, which is a continuation of business by other means, makes human virtues fatal even to their possessors. That no sacrifice is too great for the struggle against war.

Wartime involves a capitalist structure in this play. The lower classes, the peasants, the soldiers, and the traders, however, have no real way of gaining from it. If they enter willingly, like Courage, into its market, they risk its dangers. If they refuse to enter its system, they might starve--and brutal military men might take their goods whether or not they are participating.

Courage chooses to continue her involvement with the war. In Scene 7, she remains in its business dealings with gusto. Yet, if Courage were to opt out, would there be any way of her feeding her children? What Brecht presents as a lack of learning might, in the context of the Thirty Years' War, be a paradox. Nevertheless, Courage has become thoroughly a merchant, and she represents the capitalism of the war more than any common mother. She seems to have made profit her highest value--not the good things of life that money should be able to buy.

Criticism is divided about whether or not the play achieves its author's intentions, on the page or in performance. This disagreement often depends on the critical thinking that occurs in relation to the play--and in this respect, the author's broad intentions are achieved anyway.

A Stage History

Brecht, surprisingly, did not direct Mother Courage and Her Children himself in its first production in 1941. Lindtberg directed the premiere production, which played to a largely Swiss and German audience. One of those who saw this original version was Thornton Wilder. The play itself made a great impact, and Therese Giehse played the title role, yet Brecht himself felt that his intentions had been ignored, and he proceeded to work on the text to make its brutal message still clearer.

The play's most famous production to date is Brecht's own 1949 staging, which effectively was the first production of his world-famous Berliner Ensemble. Brecht himself directed this epic staging, which-with the reworked text-starred Helene Weigel in the title role. This was a show lauded by the critics, and it was given over 400 times in Berlin and across Europe. Weigel was the ultimate exponent of the Epic Theater; she embraced the contradictions of the part as well as the opportunity to display her own critical awareness of (and distaste for) some of Courage's behavior. Brecht famously recorded many of his decisions in the *Couragemodell*, a fascinating resource for anyone studying the play. Paul Dessau composed original music for the songs.

In English, it was not until the mid-1950s that Brecht really came to the notice of the British theater scene. There were two productions staged in 1955, one by Eric Capon at the Institute of Contemporary Arts, and one by Joan Littlewood with her Theatre Workshop Company. Neither made a great impact because Beckett's Waiting for Godot was stealing the theatrical limelight of 1955. Littlewood's production, seen by very few people and soon withdrawn from the repertoire, did have an important influence on her and her company, however, leading them later to adopt a markedly Brechtian mode of staging in their signature production *Oh! What a Lovely War*. It was not until 1956 that the play really came to the attention of the theater world outside Germany.

Brecht's own production came to the Palace Theatre in London in 1956, and it was met there with the famously derisive comments of Kenneth Tynan, who believed that the play was a "morality play" and thus "as tiresome as religion." The theater insiders felt differently. William Gaskill recalled later that "for many of us working in the theatre," Brecht's production "was the most important single production we have ever seen-the most influential." It was to be Gaskill's 1965 National Theatre staging that marked the first large-scale British production of the play, a production that marked, if nothing else, the fact that the play had found its way into the theatrical consciousness.

Howard Davies directed Judi Dench as Courage for the Royal Shakespeare Company in 1984 in a new version by Hanif Kureishi. This production was a popular success, but it was criticized by scholars for going against the playwright's intentions. The nightly ovations for Dench's performance made clear, it seems, that critical detachment had by no means been achieved. Glenda Jackson played Courage in the Glasgow Citizens Theatre in 1990, directed by Philip Prowse in a production that referred constantly to modern ideas of war (through video projections) and attained a Beckettian bleakness throughout.

Jonathan Kent's production at the Royal National Theatre in 1995 was of a new adaptation by major playwright David Hare, who focused very much on the way Mother Courage herself was the victim of a war that gradually silenced her. His proposed alternate title for the play was "The Silencing of Mother Courage." Diana Rigg played Courage. The production was markedly un-Brechtian, with new settings for the songs, by Jonathan Dove, and with various attempts at realism. The critical reception, thus, was mixed.

In America, Herbert Blau directed the American premiere in 1956 at the Actor's Workshop in San Francisco. Again the play was met with popular indifference and had to be called off early. The Performance Group directed a famous production in New York in 1975 that placed the audience on the stage and foregrounded contemporary references to the Vietnam War.

Recent productions have included one with Meryl Streep in a new translation by Tony Kushner in Central Park, directed by George C. Wolfe in 2006 and, for the first time, a production with a national tour of England in Stephen Unwin's lackluster production, starring Diana Quick as Courage. Unwin's bland reading of the play was slow-moving and rather painfully faithful to Brechtian practice-until, that is, the bizarre intrusion of a modern airplane sound effect came as Courage pulled her cart and the lights went down at the end.

Author of ClassicNote and Sources

Robert William, author of ClassicNote. Completed on July 30, 2007, copyright held by GradeSaver.

Updated and revised Adam Kissel August 14, 2007. Copyright held by GradeSaver.

Brecht, Bertolt (trans. Robert William). Mother Courage and Her Children. Quotations in this ClassicNote are from this edition: unpublished, 2007.

Brecht, Bertolt (trans. John Willett). Mother Courage and Her Children. London: Methuen, 1980.

Brecht, Bertolt (trans. Eric Bentley). Mother Courage and Her Children. New York: Grove, 1966.

Brecht, Bertolt. Couragemodell. Berlin: Henschelverlag, 1958.

Berlau, Ruth, et al. Theaterarbeit. Dresden: Dresdner, 1952.

Brecht, Bertolt (trans. John Willett). Brecht on Theatre. London: Methuen, 1984.

Dickson, Keith. Towards Utopia: A Study of Brecht. Oxford: Clarendon, 1988.

Fuegi, John. Bertolt Brecht: Chaos According to Plan. Cambridge: Cambridge University Press, 1987.

Thomson, Peter. Plays in Production: Mother Courage and Her Children. Cambridge: Cambridge University Press, 1997.

Thomson, Peter, and Glendyr Sacks. The Cambridge Companion to Brecht. Cambridge: Cambridge University Press, 1994.

Brecht, Bertolt. "Recordings of Brecht reading his own work." lyrikline. 2007-07-26. <http://www.lyrikline.org/index.php?id=162&L=1&author=bb01&show=Poems&cHash=500

Feldman, Adam (review of New York production in 2006). "Mother Courage and Her Children." Time Out. 2006-08-24. 2007-07-24. <http://www.timeout.com/newyork/article/5259/mother-courage-and-her-children>.

Hickling, Alfred (review of ETT production in 2006). "Mother Courage and Her Children." Guardian Unlimited. 2006-11-23. 2007-07-22. <http://arts.guardian.co.uk/reviews/story/0,,1954570,00.html>.

Essay: The Obvious in Brecht

by Lisa Cirèlle Hansson
May 30, 2001

"When something seems the most obvious thing in the world, it means that any attempt to understand the world has been given up." How does Brecht attempt to ensure that the obvious is absent from this play?

Brecht's intentions when writing Mother Courage were to communicate his beliefs and make people aware of two major issues facing society: war and capitalism. According to Brecht, people deserve the wars they get if they subscribe to a political system which is unfair and favours a specific sector of society, namely capitalism, in which it is up to the individual to secure his own means of survival. In other words, if the system is unjust in any way, war and conflict is inevitable. For this to be understood, it would be essential that the audience sees the play for what it is, as opposed to becoming engaged in its story. This means that they would have to be alienated from the play, and made perpetually aware of it as a play and nothing more. To do this, Brecht jolted audiences out of their expectations and deliberately avoided theatrical techniques that would make appearances realistic. In this way, people were forced to confront the issues at hand and decipher the meanings behind what they were being shown.

The "obvious" being referred to by Brecht is what is clearly seen, what one cannot miss. It does not require reflection and arouses no thought. By alienating the audience in this play, they see that nothing is happening at an obvious level, and can gain true understanding of the characters' reasons for behaving as they do, and of the background against which they exist.

Brecht incorporated alienation techniques in the methods of staging used in performances of Mother Courage, firstly by keeping a very bright white light trained evenly upon the set throughout. This eliminated any opportunities for creating an atmosphere; any magical or romantic views of the stage were kept strictly at bay, and no attempt was made to convey the sense of a specific place. A banner was also used to introduce every scene, as opposed to a narrator, as was most common in dramatic performances of the day. This innovative technique appeared unusual to the audience and differed from the traditional storytelling manner. Also, as words were not being spoken to them, it was difficult to get caught up in the story, as it were – to be led into an emotion by, for example, an excited tone of voice. In addition, scene changes were made in full view of the audience, reminding them of its existence as a play, again alienating them from the impression of a "true life" tale. This sense was what was intentionally put forth in other plays of the time, and one method used was to communicate the impression that a fourth wall had been cut off from the scene and that the audience was viewing incidents in the characters' lives, almost as if they were spying on them. In Brecht's play, however, this effect was dispensed with;

spectators were not intended to become involved, thus the fact that it was merely a play was constantly enforced. With regards to acting, actors were not meant to "become" their characters or persuade anyone of a transformation, they were required simply to show the character's behaviour. They did not intend to evoke empathy, but to startle the audience into objective thought. Theatrical illusion was used to the most minimal extent – stage machinery improved some representations of reality, but not enough to draw the audience out of the knowledge that they were still in a theatre. All of these methods were utilised to alienate viewers, so that they adopted and retained an attitude of inquiry and criticism in addressing the incidents and issues raised by the play, which is what epic theatre concentrated on.

Songs are frequently used in this play, and interpret the story in an objective tone. Mother Courage's first appearance on stage is initiated by a song, ensuring the audience is not empathetic, and drawing attention to it as a play from the beginning. Throughout the play, this is what the songs did, as well as make poignant observations and address real issues which Brecht wanted the audience's focus to be on. The sudden appearance of song at seemingly unlikely points in the play – when it is least expected – is alienating and can confuse an audience. Often a silly or light-hearted song would come up directly after a dramatic event, creating a lack of moral perspective and irony. Another alienating characteristic is the fact that the melodic and lyrical delivery of songs contrasts with their serious, occasionally distressing content. In the third scene, for example, the chaplain's song tells of the horrors of Christ's story, and yet the form resembles that of a nursery rhyme.

This occasional use of song makes the play difficult to define in terms of form of theatre; Brecht is mixing these forms in the same way as he does his writing style, which is both poetic and demotic. This alternating between almost romantic poetry and everyday, colloquial speech is recurrent, and the fluctuations are sudden. It is alienating that the two opposing styles are not separated in any distinct way, constantly ensuring the audience's expectations are denied.

To defer from the audience's expectations is the purpose of the play's structure – the space of time as passes unseen between the scenes is often great. After a dramatic event has surpassed, one would expect the reactions of the characters to be portrayed, or at least regarded, and the anticipated emotions to be seen, but instead one is shown occurrences of several years later. Thus, dramatic climaxes are forfeited. Also, in the same way as one cannot always see a connection between the songs and their surrounding dialogue, each scene is barely connected to the next, to the extent that the audience gets the impression that if a scene were removed, it would make little difference. There is no definite sequence of events, denying the characteristics of traditional story telling. Brecht brings in the theatre of realism by devising the play not as a convenient series of dramatic events, with a noted beginning and distinct end, for this is not what reality is. He also uses what he calls gestures, the denial of the audience's potentiality to empathise. This is an effect created by epic theatre, designed to compel the audience into remaining distanced from the story.

The methods used in this epic theatre produced an alienating effect, and deliberately separated itself from the conventional attributes of Aristotelian theatre, which appealed to the audience's emotions and evoked empathy, causing them to share the characters' feelings. Epic theatre, by definition, resolved to engage people's thinking and reasoning; Brecht objected to the soporific attitude of audiences and did not want them to be lulled into passive viewing, instead he compelled them to confront what they saw and analyse it. A significant method of alienation that ensures the audience does not get wrapped up in the suspenseful "what happens next" element of the story is Brecht's forestating – each scene is introduced with a summary of the following occurrences, establishing an inevitability which denies the audience of the passivity of viewing for the purpose of an unfolding plot. This encourages the adoption of a critical attitude, only through which understanding can be achieved. The conflicts of individual characters in Mother Courage are unimportant; the play's purpose as epic theatre is to attract the audience's attention toward more important societal issues.

The characters in the play can appear self-contradictory, which would be particularly alienating to an audience familiar solely with Aristotelian theatre. Though the characters change in this sense, no character development can be seen, and it is difficult for people to relate to them. In truth, not only would an audience be unable to empathise, but they would not know how to regard the characters. One is not given a defined set of emotions to experience, and because of the contradictions within characters, one cannot form an opinion on, or an attitude towards, them. The greatest example of this is Mother Courage herself, who is selfish and egocentric in that she subscribes to capitalist principles and is blind to their consequences. Yet, an admirable trait may be that she keeps on going through hardships and confronts danger, surviving in a man's world and ignoring her own pain for the sake of her children. However, though she disagrees with war in principle, she lacks strength of belief and exploits the war by profiting from it. The fact that she works hard – constantly, it would appear, from what we are shown of her life – but for little gain, would lead us to sympathise with her, though her deeds in the beginning of scene 3, her selling of ammunition to the opposing army, makes us question her morals. Another example of a contradictory character is the chaplain, who would be expected to condemn war and disapprove of it completely, though he said, "War satisfies all requirements, peaceable ones included, they're catered for, and it would simply fizzle out if they weren't." The chaplain can be said to have been based on contradiction – at first he was cold and formal, then later, on the battlefield, he helps the injured and shows a part of himself that is itself a victim.

What Brecht wanted to inspire in his audience was a willingness to change people's attitudes, their fixed money-centred mindsets which overshadowed, and caused confusion in, their basic moral values. According to Marx, whose principles Brecht believed in: unless man has food and shelter, he does not have freedom. This tenet is what Brecht asserts in Mother Courage, and whose understanding can only be gained when audiences realise that the obvious is an irrelevance, that this play should be seen not as a tale but as a presenting of issues. By using the aspects of character, song, structure, style, inevitability, and staging, Brecht ensures that the audience remains alienated, and that their expectations are not met.

Essay: Gender Ideals

by Geoff Cowper-Smith
June 21, 2002

"The term gender is commonly used to refer to the psychological, cultural, and social characteristics that distinguish the sexes" (Cook 1). From the idea of gender such notions as gender bias and stereotyping have developed. Stereotypes have lead society to believe that a male or female should appear, act, or in more philosophical terms, be a certain way. What these gender stereotypes are and, whether or not they really exist, will be discussed further so that they can be examined in reference to the plays Mother Courage and Her Children and M. Butterfly. In Mother Courage and Her Children "motherhood", and what it should be, is challenged as a result of the actions and qualities of the character Mother Courage. M. Butterfly gives us a great depiction of a stereotypical male, and uses the female stereotype against him. Both of these plays invert, modify, and even glorify the gender stereotypes.

Society has females and males alike typecasted into roles which have basic characteristics that are the reverse of each other. Although this has begun to change over the past thirty years, typically the man was seen as superior to the female. This superior image is one that today, is slowly on its way to being reduced to one of complete equality between the two genders.

Before the feminist revolution began, the female was traditionally in charge of taking care of the children and household. Her image in life was that of the wife, mother, and nurturing person. Some of the traits that were thought to be uniquely feminine were; ". . .emotional, sensitive, gentle, quiet, nurturing, interested in personal appearance and beauty, focused upon home and family. . ." (3). Generally the image of the woman was quiet, submissive, and dedicated towards the well-being of her family.

> "The stereotypical role for women is to focus their lives on marriage, home and children. They rely on men for sustenance and status. The expectancy is that women will engage in nurturing and life preserving activities through childbearing and caretaking behaviors. Additionally, there is also emphasis on personal appearance and prohibition on direct expression of aggression, assertion, and striving for power." (qtd. in Cook 59)

The stereotypical male image was the complete opposite to that of the female one. Men were seen as the leaders of the household, the money-makers, and rational thinkers. Their characteristics were seen as; ". . .aggressive, unemotional, objective, dominant, competitive, logical/rational, decisive, assertive, analytical, strong, sexual, physical, successful. . ." (2). Men were the protectors of their families and were responsible for providing the strength which the family would need to survive. They did not like to have their judgement questioned or be instructed how to act.

> "The stereotypical role for men includes emphasizing physical strength and achievement, restricting emotions (except anger), avoiding emotional intimacy with same-sex peers, and providing sustenance and protection for women and children." (qtd. in Cook 59)

These ideals for what men and women should be certainly left men with more power and women with a responsibility to keep out of the way. As it was briefly touched upon earlier, the plays Mother Courage and Her Children and M. Butterfly reverse or glorify these stereotypes that have been attributed to the two genders.

The character of Mother Courage in Mother Courage and Her Children has personality traits that are far from those stereotypically defined as feminine. In fact, if her characteristics and actions are examined closely, she seems to have assumed those of a male. She tries to help her children survive the thirty years war. While looking after them is typically a female quality and responsibility, doing so by running a small business and welcoming a war rather than running from it, is much more masculine. She received the name Courage, after driving her cart of bread straight through the middle of a military bombardment because she was broke and her bread was going moldy. This is hardly the action of someone who isn't supposed to be assertive or strive for power. Women aren't supposed to be responsible for generating money for the family to survive on, but Courage did so ruthlessly. At one point she was so pre-occupied with trying to save money that one of her sons, Swiss Cheese, ends up being executed because she tried to bargain with his captors. Even then, his death doesn't bring out any feminine emotion in her; she just keeps on pushing, trying to survive. At the end of the play, when the last of her children are dead, Courage still keeps on going. She picks up her cart without a second thought and moves on by herself. Whereas conversely, the typical woman would be drowned in emotion, Mother Courage's reaction is that of a stereotypical male.

Mother Courage is a character who very matter-of-factly makes a statement. Women are capable of achieving exactly that which men do. Women and war are images not traditionally related. Perhaps, if any relation can be drawn during a war, it is that women are waiting for their men to come home from defending their honour. Mother Courage shows us that if a woman is put in such a situation of conflict and disparity she too can survive; although by doing so she takes on those ideal masculine qualities. These qualities are displayed throughout the entire play, and the only time we see the true feminine motherliness in Courage is when a recruiter tries to get her boys to enlist. She immediately tries to convince him that he ought to ignore them. Her boys aren't up for trade. This motherly protectiveness is supposedly typical of women. As quoted from Cook, ". . .women will engage in nurturing and life preserving activities. . ." (59). However we quickly see Mother Courage revert to her male characteristics as the recruiter decides to keep pressing the issue of her sons enlistment. She suddenly pulls a knife on the man and says: "Go on, you kidnap him, just try. I'll slit you open, trash" (Brecht 1.1.184-185). Protectiveness is one thing, but sheer aggression is categorized as a male trait. Mother Courage is a physical force to be reckoned with and that force is not a quality indicative of a stereotypical woman.

M. Butterfly depicts a man, Gallimard, as a possessor of completely typical, ideal masculine qualities. He is the male stereotype. In this play the female stereotype is what destroys him. The girl Gallimard meets and falls in love with, Song, portrays the ideal female so perfectly that Gallimard can't fathom the idea, or at the very least deny that she could be a spy; let alone a male actor.

The male actor knows exactly how to get Gallimard to pursue Song. He creates a girl who is so fragile that Gallimard immediately finds a desire to protect her in his arms. Song starts to draw Gallimard in when she calls him at 5:30 in the morning and tells him "I waited until I saw the sun. That was as much discipline as I could manage for one night. Do you forgive me?" (Hwang 1.9.76-77) She is appealing to Gallimard's sexual and dominant characteristics because the stereotypical man enjoys the idea of a woman who is desperate for his attention. Song plays on Gallimard's need for dominance, and puts him on a pedestal. She acts quiet, and frightened. She even tells him that she has never invited a man into her flat before - which spurns Gallimard's interest as to whether or not she's even been with a man before. His dominant and competitive traits make him want to be her first sexual partner. The male actor has achieved exactly what he wants with Song when Gallimard states that he thinks she feels inferior to him (1.10.90).

Gallimard stops calling and seeing Song as he wants to make her even more desperate for him. The male actor, Song, plays right along and after six weeks begins to write a series of letters which finally end with telling Gallimard that she has given him her shame - what else could he want? (1.11.90) Gallimard's stereotypical male reaction is a feeling of power from the process of ignoring her. ". . .I stopped going to the opera, I didn't phone or write her. I knew this little flower was waiting for me to call, and, as I wickedly refused to do so, I felt for the first time that rush of poweróthat absolute power of a man" (1.11.10). Never does Gallimard find this a little too simple, or his Song too perfect. In fact her perfection encourages him to brag that he found the perfect woman (1.3.5). Of course his perfect woman turns out to be a cross-dressing, male, Chinese informant.

The illusions are destroyed and Gallimard's dream shattered when he learns the truth about Song, and consequently the mythical existence of "the perfect woman". Instead he only realizes the reality of the stereotypical male qualities he possesses. Near the end of the play when Gallimard laughingly points out that he finds humor in the amount of time he wasted on ". . .just a man" (3.2.99) it's really quite ironic that his attitude for the entire play could have been summed up as "just a girl." He obviously didn't find her to be a challenge, he openly decided that she was inferior to him. It would have been much more logical for him to shake the actor's hand out of masculine respect when the truth was revealed.

Mother Courage and Her Children inverts the stereotypical female ideal and gives the character Mother Courage glorified male characteristics. This play creates a glimpse of gender equality. Mother Courage is capable of exactly that which men are. She becomes even more powerful than the typical man by retaining that motherly quality of looking out for the children and by doing so in an aggressive, masculine manner. So aggressive that she ends up losing her offsprings. Mother Courage and Her Children raises the question: "what would happen if both genders possessed male stereotypical traits?"

The male stereotype, Gallimard, is destroyed by the idea of the"Perfect Woman" (1.3.5) in M. Butterfly. The play shatters the illusion of the female ideal. The character Gallimard discovers that it doesn't really exist. However, the stereotypical male all too real. It is glorified to its absolute extremes in this play.

The one conclusion that can be drawn between these two plays and gender stereotypes, is that stereotypical masculine characteristics are quite genuine. Conversely, those qualities that create the female ideal, are merely a figment of male perceptions.

Works Cited

Brecht, Bertolt. "Mother Courage and Her Children." Worthen 727-751.

Cook, Ellen Piel, ed. Women, Relationships, and Power. Virginia: American Counseling Association, 1993.

Hwang, Henry David. "M. Butterfly." Worthen 1062-1084.

Worthen, W.B. ed. The Harcourt Brace Anthology of Drama. 3rd ed. Toronto: Harcourt, 1993.

Quiz 1

1. **What are the dates of the Second World War?**
    A. 1612-1616
    B. 1940-1943
    C. 1939-1941
    D. 1939-1945

2. **Where was Brecht when he wrote Mother Courage and Her Children?**
    A. Sweden
    B. Germany
    C. Austria
    D. Switzerland

3. **What was the theater form that Brecht founded?**
    A. Post-War Theater
    B. Dramatic Theater
    C. In-Yer-Face Theater
    D. Epic Theater

4. **When was Brecht's own first major production of Mother Courage?**
    A. 1937
    B. 1939
    C. 1941
    D. 1949

5. **During which war is Mother Courage and Her Children set?**
    A. The Crimean War
    B. The First World War
    C. The Second World War
    D. The Thirty Years' War

6. **What is Mother Courage's real name?**
    A. Kattrin Haupt
    B. Anne Doubtfire
    C. Adolf Hitler
    D. Anna Fierling

7. **What is the name of Mother Courage's only daughter?**
   A. Doris Lessing
   B. Kattrin
   C. Eilif
   D. Swiss Cheese

8. **How did the protagonist get the nickname "Mother Courage"?**
   A. By driving through a bombardment to sell some moldy bread
   B. By being the only woman to help fight off a Catholic invasion
   C. By singing numerous difficult songs in public
   D. By selling her cart to save her son

9. **Which child is Mother Courage's favorite?**
   A. The Cook
   B. Kattrin
   C. Eilif
   D. Swiss Cheese

10. **How does Mother Courage predict the Sergeant's death in the play's first scene?**
   A. By making him draw a black cross on a piece of paper
   B. By reading his tea leaves
   C. By seeing into the future
   D. By finding a mystic symbol drawn on his uniform

11. **Which of Mother Courage's children works as a paymaster?**
   A. Kattrin
   B. The Chaplain
   C. Eilif
   D. Swiss Cheese

12. **Who played Mother Courage in the 1949 production?**
   A. Diana Rigg
   B. Judi Dench
   C. Diana Quick
   D. Helene Weigel

13. **How many of Mother Courage's children die by the end of the play?**

A. Eilif and Swiss Cheese (2)
B. Only Eilif (1)
C. All of them (3)
D. Swiss Cheese and Kattrin (2)

14. **What is the Cook's real name?**

A. Chicken
B. Lamb
C. Fish
D. Pork

15. **What is the Cook's nickname as revealed by Yvette?**

A. Puff the Magic Dragon
B. Peter the Puff
C. Smoking Steven
D. Smoked Lamb

16. **What is Yvette Pottier's occupation?**

A. Chaplain
B. Cook
C. Seamstress
D. Prostitute

17. **What does Yvette Pottier wear that Kattrin later steals?**

A. Hat and red high-heeled boots
B. Soldier's Uniform
C. Lederhosen
D. Scarf

18. **How does Kattrin attempt to awake the townsfolk in Scene 11?**

A. Banging a drum
B. Shooting a harquebus
C. Shouting loudly
D. Chopping a tree with an axe

19. **What is Brecht's first name?**
   A. Bertie
   B. Robert
   C. Bertolt
   D. Bertholt

20. **When did Brecht die?**
   A. 1941
   B. 1945
   C. 1950
   D. 1956

21. **Which regiment is Courage following at the start of the play?**
   A. Second German
   B. First Swedish
   C. Second Finnish
   D. Ninth Augustan

22. **What is Eilif's surname?**
   A. Kojocki
   B. Lojocki
   C. Mojocki
   D. Nojocki

23. **How does Courage protect her children in the first scene?**
   A. By pretending to be a soldier
   B. By lying about their places of birth
   C. By running away in her cart
   D. By drawing a knife on the soldiers

24. **What disability does Kattrin have?**
   A. She cannot walk
   B. She is deaf
   C. She is dumb
   D. She is blind

25. **How much does the Cook end up paying for Courage's capon in Scene 2?**

A. Nine Guilders

B. Sixty Hellers

C. Forty dollars

D. One florin

Quiz 1 Answer Key

1. **(D)** 1939-1945
2. **(A)** Sweden
3. **(D)** Epic Theater
4. **(D)** 1949
5. **(D)** The Thirty Years' War
6. **(D)** Anna Fierling
7. **(B)** Kattrin
8. **(A)** By driving through a bombardment to sell some moldy bread
9. **(C)** Eilif
10. **(A)** By making him draw a black cross on a piece of paper
11. **(D)** Swiss Cheese
12. **(D)** Helene Weigel
13. **(C)** All of them (3)
14. **(B)** Lamb
15. **(B)** Peter the Puff
16. **(D)** Prostitute
17. **(A)** Hat and red high-heeled boots
18. **(A)** Banging a drum
19. **(C)** Bertolt
20. **(D)** 1956
21. **(C)** Second Finnish
22. **(D)** Nojocki
23. **(D)** By drawing a knife on the soldiers
24. **(C)** She is dumb
25. **(D)** One florin

Quiz 2

1. **What is the General's favorite wine in Scene 2?**
   A. Merlot
   B. Chablis
   C. Falernian
   D. Chardonnay

2. **What is the heroic deed for which Eilif is rewarded in Scene 2?**
   A. Slaughtering peasants in order to steal their cattle
   B. Hiding the regiment's cash box
   C. Shooting Kattrin off a thatched roof
   D. Burning down a farm

3. **What is the official reason for the war being fought?**
   A. Religion
   B. Terrorism
   C. Territory
   D. Money

4. **Why does Courage think the General in Scene 2 is a bad general?**
   A. Because he advocates looting
   B. Because a good general would have no need of weapons
   C. Because a good general would have no need of courageous men
   D. Because he drinks too much

5. **Which song does Eilif sing in Scene 2?**
   A. The Song of the Hours
   B. The Song of the Girl and the Soldier
   C. The Song of Tomorrow
   D. The Song of the Great Capitulation

6. **What happens to the soldier at the end of the song of the Girl and the Soldier?**
   A. He is shot
   B. He drowns
   C. He kills a peasant
   D. He marries the girl

7. **What does Eilif do while singing the song of the Girl and the Soldier?**
    A. Upturns the table
    B. Dances a war-dance with his saber
    C. Drinks the wine the General has poured for him
    D. Embraces his mother

8. **At the start of Scene 3, what is the Armorer attempting to sell Courage?**
    A. A cannon
    B. Four officers' shirts
    C. Armor
    D. A sack of shot

9. **For how much does Courage buy the sack of shot in Scene 3?**
    A. Sixty Hellers
    B. One and a half florins
    C. One florin
    D. Two florins

10. **Why does the Cook get the nickname "Peter the Puff"?**
    A. Because he takes snuff
    B. Because he is gay
    C. Because he hates the name
    D. Because during sex he does not remove his pipe from his mouth

11. **Which song does Yvette sing in Scene 3?**
    A. The Song of the Hours
    B. The Song of Tomorrow
    C. The Song of the Great Capitulation
    D. The Song of Fraternization

12. **What does Kattrin do while Courage, the Cook, and the Chaplain discuss the King's actions in Poland?**
    A. Polishes the glasses
    B. Places Courage's skirt on top of the Cook's trousers
    C. Tries on Yvette's shoes and imitates her walk
    D. Sings a song

13. **What is the Song of Fraternization about?**

A. Kattrin's longing for a marriage partner
B. Yvette's relationship with "Peter the Puff"
C. Courage's relationship with the Cook
D. Brotherhood between soldiers

14. **What does the Chaplain do when the Catholics invade?**

A. Takes off his clerical robes
B. Prepares to fight, loading the cannon
C. Sings a hymn with Kattrin
D. Prays

15. **How does Courage attempt to make Kattrin less attractive when the Catholics invade in Scene 3?**

A. Covers her face in ashes and removes Yvette's shoes
B. Makes her smoke the pipe
C. Disguises her as Yvette
D. Covers her face in ashes and disguises her as Yvette

16. **Where does Swiss Cheese suggest putting the cashbox when the Catholics invade in Scene 3?**

A. In the bin
B. In Courage's cart
C. Under his jumper
D. In the river

17. **Who comes looking for Swiss Cheese after the Catholics have invaded?**

A. General Tilly
B. A man with an eyepatch
C. A spy from the Protestant camp
D. Napoleon Bonaparte

18. **What is the Chaplain's real name?**

A. We are never told--he is only referred to as "Chaplain"
B. Alastair Roberts
C. Charles Wolf
D. Russell Kirk

19. **What is the Song of the Hours about?**
    A. Christ's Passion
    B. The value of watches and clocks
    C. Kattrin's long hours on the cart
    D. The passage of time

20. **Whom does Yvette enter with in Scene 3?**
    A. A very old, very rich Colonel
    B. The Cook
    C. The Recrutiing Officer
    D. The Chaplain

21. **What does Yvette want to buy from Courage?**
    A. Her officers' shirts
    B. Brandy
    C. Her cart
    D. Her daughter

22. **What does Courage suggest that Yvette do instead of buying her cart outright?**
    A. Mortgaging it to her
    B. Destroying it
    C. Hiding it
    D. Borrowing it for a while

23. **What is Courage's initial offer to bribe the soldiers not to kill Swiss Cheese?**
    A. Two hundred florins
    B. Sixty Hellers
    C. One hundred twenty florins
    D. One hundred fifty florins

24. **According to Courage, "Bribery in humans is like" what?**
    A. Jesus' suffering
    B. Virtue in humans
    C. German cake
    D. Mercy in God

25. **What do Courage and Kattrin do while waiting to hear whether their bribe has saved Swiss Cheese?**
    A. Smash glasses
    B. Polish knives
    C. Pray
    D. Start fires

Quiz 2 Answer Key

1. **(C)** Falernian
2. **(A)** Slaughtering peasants in order to steal their cattle
3. **(A)** Religion
4. **(C)** Because a good general would have no need of courageous men
5. **(B)** The Song of the Girl and the Soldier
6. **(B)** He drowns
7. **(B)** Dances a war-dance with his saber
8. **(D)** A sack of shot
9. **(B)** One and a half florins
10. **(D)** Because during sex he does not remove his pipe from his mouth
11. **(D)** The Song of Fraternization
12. **(C)** Tries on Yvette's shoes and imitates her walk
13. **(B)** Yvette's relationship with "Peter the Puff"
14. **(A)** Takes off his clerical robes
15. **(A)** Covers her face in ashes and removes Yvette's shoes
16. **(B)** In Courage's cart
17. **(B)** A man with an eyepatch
18. **(A)** We are never told--he is only referred to as "Chaplain"
19. **(A)** Christ's Passion
20. **(A)** A very old, very rich Colonel
21. **(C)** Her cart
22. **(A)** Mortgaging it to her
23. **(C)** One hundred twenty florins
24. **(D)** Mercy in God
25. **(B)** Polish knives

Quiz 3

1. **What does Courage do when asked if she knows the recently deceased Swiss Cheese?**
   A. She only laughs
   B. She just shakes her head
   C. She says, "Get him out of here!"
   D. She asks for the body

2. **What is the Clerk's advice to Mother Courage at the start of Scene 4?**
   A. Don't complain
   B. Always trade for the best price
   C. Only complain if you are angry enough for it not to wear out
   D. Complain as bitterly as possible

3. **Which song does Courage sing in Scene 4?**
   A. The Song of the Adulterated Capitalist
   B. The Song of the Hours
   C. The Song of Tomorrow
   D. The Song of the Great Capitulation

4. **What is the Song of the Great Capitulation about?**
   A. Kattrin's repressed sexual urges
   B. Soldiers sleeping with civilians
   C. How everyone will eventually succumb to the war
   D. Christ's suffering on the cross

5. **What does the young soldier at the end of Scene 4 do?**
   A. Stays and complains to the Captain
   B. Exits, shouting abuse, but not complaining
   C. Attacks Mother Courage
   D. Slaughters peasants and steals their cattle

6. **What does Courage do at the end of Scene 4?**
   A. Decides not to complain
   B. Screams silently
   C. Sings the Song of the Hours
   D. Sings the Song of the Great Capitulation

7. **What does Tilly's victory at Magdeburg cost Courage?**
   A. Four officers' shirts
   B. Thirty hellers
   C. A daughter
   D. A son

8. **What is the Chaplain doing during the shooting in Scene 5?**
   A. Praying
   B. Rescuing peasants from out of the gunfire
   C. Chopping firewood
   D. Polishing glasses

9. **Complete the line: "I have no soul. But I do need ____"**
   A. Brandy
   B. Firewood
   C. Officers' shirts
   D. Brimstone

10. **What does Kattrin rescue from the gunfire in Scene 5?**
   A. A cannon
   B. Her drum
   C. Assorted wares, bought by her mother
   D. A baby

11. **Why does the Chaplain take Courage's officers' shirts from her?**
   A. To sell on to the army
   B. To use as bandages to aid the injured
   C. To wear himself
   D. To fuel the fire he is kindling

12. **How was the General Tilly killed?**
   A. Shot by the enemy when he rode in their direction, having been confused by a fog
   B. Poisoned
   C. Executed for holding the regimental paybox
   D. Shot off a roof when banging a drum

13. **What is Courage doing during General Tilly's funeral?**
   A. Singing the Song of the Hours
   B. Drinking
   C. A stock check
   D. A dance

14. **Complete the line: "What becomes of the hole, when ____"**
   A. The cork has been lost
   B. The parts have been destroyed
   C. The cheese has been eaten
   D. The people have been killed

15. **What does Courage decide as a result of talking to the Chaplain in Scene 6?**
   A. To sell everything she owns
   B. To buy new stock
   C. Not to buy any new stock
   D. To buy half her usual stock

16. **What does the Chaplain do while complaining to Courage about his clerical role in Scene 6?**
   A. Chops firewood
   B. Polishes knives
   C. Polishes glasses
   D. Sings The Song of the Hours

17. **What happens to Kattrin when she is sent to fetch merchandise in Scene 6?**
   A. She is assaulted and badly wounded
   B. She has all the merchandise stolen from her
   C. She is shot
   D. She is attacked and killed

18. **What does Kattrin do when Courage gives her the red boots, after Kattrin has been assaulted?**
   A. Smashes two brandy glasses
   B. Leaves them where they are, and crawls into the cart
   C. Puts them on and imitates Yvette's walk
   D. Sings the Song of the Hours

19. **What does Courage do at the end of Scene 7, following Kattrin's assault?**
   A. Curses the war
   B. Praises the war
   C. Buys more merchandise
   D. Harnesses herself up ready to start moving

20. **In Scene 7, how is Mother Courage's business going?**
   A. very well
   B. to the dogs
   C. very badly
   D. reasonably

21. **What are the peasants trying to sell Courage in Scene 8?**
   A. Brandy
   B. Bedding
   C. Shot
   D. A harquebus

22. **What is the reaction of the old woman when she learns that peace has broken out?**
   A. She cheers and dances
   B. She sings the Song of the Hours
   C. She faints
   D. She screams

23. **Why does the Cook return to the play in Scene 8?**
   A. Because he wants to do some looting
   B. Because the regiment has not paid him
   C. Because he is bored
   D. Because he has been sacked

24. **What does the Chaplain call Courage when he loses his temper with her?**
   A. The Cook's accomplice
   B. A leopard
   C. The devil's spoon
   D. A hyena of the battlefield

25. **When Yvette returns to the play in Scene 8, she is...**

A. In a wheelchair
B. Dumb
C. Severely wounded
D. Older and much fatter, heavily powdered

Quiz 3 Answer Key

1. **(B)** She just shakes her head
2. **(A)** Don't complain
3. **(D)** The Song of the Great Capitulation
4. **(C)** How everyone will eventually succumb to the war
5. **(B)** Exits, shouting abuse, but not complaining
6. **(A)** Decides not to complain
7. **(A)** Four officers' shirts
8. **(B)** Rescuing peasants from out of the gunfire
9. **(B)** Firewood
10. **(D)** A baby
11. **(B)** To use as bandages to aid the injured
12. **(A)** Shot by the enemy when he rode in their direction, having been confused by a fog
13. **(C)** A stock check
14. **(C)** The cheese has been eaten
15. **(B)** To buy new stock
16. **(A)** Chops firewood
17. **(A)** She is assaulted and badly wounded
18. **(B)** Leaves them where they are, and crawls into the cart
19. **(A)** Curses the war
20. **(A)** very well
21. **(B)** Bedding
22. **(C)** She faints
23. **(B)** Because the regiment has not paid him
24. **(D)** A hyena of the battlefield
25. **(D)** Older and much fatter, heavily powdered

Quiz 4

1. **Where is the tavern that the Cook inherits?**
    A. Berlin
    B. Alchten
    C. Utrecht
    D. Magdeburg

2. **What is the only thing growing, according to Courage in Scene 9?**
    A. Strawberries
    B. Brambles
    C. Wheat
    D. Grass

3. **Why does Courage retract her initial agreement to go with the Cook to Utrecht?**
    A. Because Kattrin cannot come along
    B. Because Utrecht is too far away
    C. Because peace breaks out
    D. Because the Chaplain refuses to accompany her

4. **Who are the great men mentioned in the Song of Solomon?**
    A. Solomon, Julius Caesar, Socrates, Saint Martin
    B. Augustine, Julius Caesar, Caligula, Saint Martin
    C. Solomon, General Tilly, Augustine
    D. Solomon, Martin Luther King, Stalin

5. **What does Kattrin attempt to do after overhearing the Cook's refusal to take her to Utrecht?**
    A. Escapes, only to be shot by soldiers
    B. Climbs onto the roof and bangs a drum
    C. Packs to leave, and provocatively leaves Courage's skirt and Cook's trousers on the wheel of the cart
    D. Attempts to collect some merchandise

6. **What do the peasants do on hearing that the soldiers are going to storm the town of Halle?**
    A. Attempt to smash up Mother Courage's cart
    B. Raise the alarm to awake the townspeople
    C. Sing the Song of the Hours
    D. Pray, after defending their own failure to act

7. **What prompts Kattrin to climb onto the roof in Scene 11?**
   A. The noise of the drum
   B. The peasants mentioning the young children asleep in the town
   C. Gunfire from afar
   D. The soldiers exiting towards the town

8. **Why does Kattrin bang the drum on the roof?**
   A. To stop the peasants from praying
   B. To accompany Mother Courage's song
   C. To awake the townsfolk
   D. To make some noise

9. **What stops Kattrin from banging the drum?**
   A. She falls off the roof
   B. The townspeople awake
   C. Gunfire from afar
   D. She is shot by the soldiers

10. **What happens at the end of Scene 11, following Kattrin's death?**
   A. The house burns down
   B. Noise from the town indicates that the people have been woken up
   C. The soldiers flee
   D. Mother Courage returns to find her body

11. **What is significant about Mother Courage's lullaby to Kattrin?**
   A. It gets Kattrin's name wrong
   B. The tune is the same as The Song of the Hours
   C. It is highly materialistic and competitive
   D. Courage is unable to finish singing it

12. **What does Courage do before paying for Kattrin's burial?**
   A. Closes Kattrin's eyes
   B. Takes back the jewellery Kattrin is wearing
   C. Scatters ash over Kattrin's body
   D. Fetches a tarpaulin from the cart and covers Kattrin with it

13. **What does Courage say before following the regiment at the very end of the play?**
   A. The war be damned
   B. I can't think about Kattrin now
   C. Give me my reward!
   D. I've got to get back into business

14. **What did Brecht want his audience primarily to do when in the theater?**
   A. Join in with the play
   B. Observe with critical detachment
   C. Laugh
   D. Get emotionally involved

15. **Which term best describes Brecht?**
   A. Buddhist
   B. Christian
   C. socialist
   D. capitalist

16. **Who was the first person ever to play Mother Courage in the premiere production in Zurich?**
   A. Monika Moerat
   B. Therese Giehse
   C. Bertolt Brecht
   D. Helene Weigel

17. **What did Helene Weigel do, playing Courage, at the end of Scene 3?**
   A. Silently stood up and exited
   B. Screamed
   C. Silently fainted
   D. Screamed silently

18. **How did Brecht's audiences know the locations of the scenes?**
   A. Large photographs were projected onto the back wall of the set
   B. Placards or "scene headings" with locations written on them were flown in as part of the set
   C. Someone always announced the locations in the first few lines
   D. The actors adopted regional accents

19. **Who does Yvette eventually marry?**
   A. The Cook
   B. The Colonel she enters with in Scene 3
   C. The brother of the Colonel she enters with in Scene 3
   D. The Chaplain

20. **Which word did Brecht use to mean "making the audience critically aware"?**
   A. Amelioration
   B. Dramatization
   C. Criticalization
   D. Alienation

21. **What does the German term "Verfremdung" mean?**
   A. Historicization or "to portray history"
   B. Dramatization or "to make emotional"
   C. Alienation or "to make strange"
   D. Exclusion or "to identify by negation"

22. **The play, according to Brecht, is a ____ of the Thirty Years' War:**
   A. Dramatization
   B. Vignette
   C. Chronicle
   D. Basic Record

23. **Who was Brecht's original composer for Mother Courage?**
   A. Ralph Manheim
   B. Kurt Weill
   C. Stephen Sondheim
   D. Paul Dessau

24. **Which is the longest scene in the play?**
   A. Scene 3
   B. Scene 4
   C. Scene 7
   D. Scene 12

25. **Which scene consists only of a song?**

A. Scene 10
B. Scene 11
C. Scene 12
D. Scene 14

Quiz 4 Answer Key

1. **(C)** Utrecht
2. **(B)** Brambles
3. **(A)** Because Kattrin cannot come along
4. **(A)** Solomon, Julius Caesar, Socrates, Saint Martin
5. **(C)** Packs to leave, and provocatively leaves Courage's skirt and Cook's trousers on the wheel of the cart
6. **(D)** Pray, after defending their own failure to act
7. **(B)** The peasants mentioning the young children asleep in the town
8. **(C)** To awake the townsfolk
9. **(D)** She is shot by the soldiers
10. **(B)** Noise from the town indicates that the people have been woken up
11. **(C)** It is highly materialistic and competitive
12. **(D)** Fetches a tarpaulin from the cart and covers Kattrin with it
13. **(D)** I've got to get back into business
14. **(B)** Observe with critical detachment
15. **(C)** socialist
16. **(B)** Therese Giehse
17. **(D)** Screamed silently
18. **(B)** Placards or "scene headings" with locations written on them were flown in as part of the set
19. **(C)** The brother of the Colonel she enters with in Scene 3
20. **(D)** Alienation
21. **(C)** Alienation or "to make strange"
22. **(C)** Chronicle
23. **(D)** Paul Dessau
24. **(A)** Scene 3
25. **(A)** Scene 10

Quiz 5

1. **How many scenes are there in Mother Courage and Her Children?**
   A. 10
   B. 11
   C. 12
   D. 16

2. **What language was this play originally written in?**
   A. German
   B. English
   C. Swedish
   D. French

Quiz 5 Answer Key

1. **(C)** 12
2. **(A)** German

ClassicNotes

GradeSaver™

Getting you the grade since 1999™

Other ClassicNotes from GradeSaver™

Waiting for Lefty
Walden
Washington Square
Where the Red Fern Grows
White Fang
White Noise
White Teeth
Who's Afraid of Virginia Woolf
Wide Sargasso Sea
Winesburg, Ohio
The Winter's Tale
Woyzeck
Wuthering Heights
The Yellow Wallpaper
Yonnondio: From the Thirties

473952

Made in the USA